Early American Almanac Humor

Early American Almanac Humor

Robert K. Dodge

Bowling Green State University Popular Press

Bowling Green, Ohio 43403

Cover design by Gary Dumm

Library of Congress Catalogue Card No.: 87-70546
Copyright © 1987 by Bowling Green State University Popular Press

ISBN: 0-87972-393-3 Clothbound
         0-87972-394-7 Paperback

Acknowledgements:

The following institution and individuals have been of great assistance in the completion of this work.

The late Mody Boatright who first suggested the topic, the University of Nevada, Las Vegas which provided me with a sabbatical leave and with research assistance, Constance Simpson-Blau, Dennis McBride and especially Raynette Lee for their assistance with the preliminary research, Michael Stitt and Joseph McCullough, two colleagues, for their advice and support, and Leslie Dodge for her love, advice and support.

Contents

Introduction

No one knows to what extent the first Americans in Roanoke, Jamestown and Plymouth told each other comic stories and jokes. We do know that during the early years of the American colonies comparatively little humor was written down or published. William Byrd, Thomas Merton of Merrymount and Stephen Burroughs were three of our only colonial writers of humor.

At the same time that written American humor failed to take hold, almanacs were flourishing in the colonies. Stephen Daye printed America's first almanac in 1639 in Cambridge, Massachusetts. For the next two and a half centuries almanacs played an important part in American life. Hundreds of almanacs were published in our largest cities and in many of our smallest towns. Peddlers carried them into parts of the country that were not served by booksellers. Farmers, shippers and fishermen often felt that they needed an almanac in order to regulate their yearly activities. Publishers of almanacs believed that they had a guaranteed annual market, and they were right. Americans would buy almanacs, the important question was whose almanacs would they buy?

The earliest almanac makers competed with each other, but the earliest almanacs were usually little more than a calendar and, until the second quarter of the eighteenth century, the calendar pages dominated almost every published almanac. Competition between almanac publishers depended on their claims as to the accuracy of their calendars.

Nathaniel Ames and James Franklin, publishers of two of America's first best-selling almanacs can be credited with the beginning of a different kind of competition. They realized that the accuracy of the calendar could only be pushed so far as a sales inducement, and they began to include other material in their almanacs, material that they hoped would increase their sales. Ames often included short paragraphs on current events and morality. James Franklin invented the character of Poor Robin who gave his readers the sayings of Poor Robin.

Ames and James Franklin changed the rules of almanac competition, but it was James' brother Benjamin who carried the process to its first fruition. Benjamin Franklin's first almanac burst upon the Philadelphia scene with the creation of Poor Richard and the prediction of the death of Titan Leeds, at the time the most popular almanac maker in the city. The world of almanacs

1

would be permanently changed. *Poor Richard's Almanack* became the best selling American almanac ever published. Other almanac makers began to copy it.

When other almanac publishers saw what non-calendar material had done for the sales of *Poor Richard*, many wasted little time in adding material of their own. In the decades following the introduction of *Poor Richard*, almanacs grew longer and longer as publishers competed to find more and more material that would induce the public to buy their almanacs. It is such material that makes eighteenth and nineteenth century almanacs so interesting to the student of early American popular culture. Among other materials are hundreds of "valuable receipts" for improving soil, increasing crop yields, curing diseases in livestock and humans and for the preparation and preservation of food. Many almanacs contain descriptions of such American customs as bundling, bees and peddling. Stories and essays also appeared. By the last half of the eighteenth century, many almanacs had begun to provide pure information in the style of the present-day *World Almanac and Book of Facts*.

The competitive almanac makers did not take long to realize that Franklin's humor made his almanacs sell, and they began to use all kinds of comic items to give potential buyers an additional reason to buy their almanacs rather than another. Purely comic almanacs did not flourish until the nineteenth century, but many of the serious almanacs of the late eighteenth century contained from one to as many as a dozen anecdotes or other comic items, much as such magazines as *The Reader's Digest* include comic items along with their more serious material. Between 1776 and 1800 more than 2,000 comic items (including duplications) were published in serious American almanacs. At last there was a source of written popular humor. In fact, the serious almanacs of the late eighteenth century are the most important source of popular humor available to us before the comic almanacs and journals of the nineteenth century.

The humor of such almanacs has never been collected or studied in any systematic fashion. George Lyman Kittredge published an excellent study of the almanacs of Robert B. Thomas,[1] Robb Sagendorph's *America and Her Almanacs: Wit, Wisdom and Weather* does not attempt to give much analysis of almanac humor.[2] Marion Barber Stowell studied some 450 almanacs of the seventeenth and eighteenth centuries and produced a scholarly work, but she paid little attention to almanac humor.[3]

Only three articles have dealt specifically with almanac humor from the late eighteenth century. In 1971 *The Journal of Popular Culture* published my article on didactic almanac humor.[4] *Indian Historian* published an article by Jon Stanley Wenrick that used almanac anecdotes as important source material[5] and *Eire-Ireland* published my article on the Irish comic stereotype in the humor of almanacs of this period.[6]

That almanac humor from 1776-1800 has been so little studied is not attributable to its lack of importance. Rather, almanac humor is obscure and scattered throughout more than a thousand sources, each of which must be examined page by page. Moreover, it is only when one has collected it for some time that a concept of its volume can be grasped. The scattered nature of the comic items makes it appear that the total number will be rather small. Instead, there are more than two thousand items, and they suggest much about the way American humor developed in the years of the early republic (1776-1800). Obviously there is a need for a work such as the present one, a work which gathers many of the comic items together and makes them available to scholars of American humor, to students and to those who appreciate a joke that is so old they may never have heard it.

The almanac humor of early America is important partly because of a phenomenon mentioned by Mark Twain and exemplified by a story reported by Richard Dorson. A Yankee, it is told, tricked a group of hostile Indians by bragging about his abilities as a medicine man. When they refused to believe him, he first took out his false teeth and then removed his false leg. "The terrified Indians still standing their ground, the desperate Yankee took his head in both hands and made a move as if to unscrew it and lay it on the ground..." He also told the Indians that he could do the same to them. They fled.[7]

The story appears as an essentially American tale. It has an American setting (the great plains), it deals with American characters (the Yankee and the Indians) and it fits the form of the exaggerated trickster tale associated with the American frontier. In fact it is an American tale, but a similar tale with a British setting and British characters appeared in print in an American almanac considerably before the first appearance of the Indian and Yankee tale.

The Virginia Almanac, for...1799 printed an anecdote about Sam Foote, a well-known eighteenth century British comic actor who is mentioned several times in Boswell's *Life of Johnson*. According to the almanac, Foote gathered together a number of people who wore prosthetic devices and went on a tour of the English countryside. Each evening they would stop at a public house and eat and drink their fill. They would then begin frightening the landlord by removing their limbs, noses and eyes. Foote, himself, would ask the landlord to remove his boot and the landlord would be surprised to find that Foote's leg came off with his boot. Finally, one of the company would ask the landlord to lift off his head for him. The landlord, believing them to be devils, then would kick them all out of the house refusing to touch their money. The free service, of course, was the object of Foote's deception.[8]

It is impossible to assume that the Foote anecdote is the original of the Indian-Yankee tale. The two stories may have derived from different sources, or one or both may have originated with no source at all. The similarity of the final gesture of pretending to remove one's head after removing other bodily parts constitutes the closest correspondence between the two stories and may indicate some relationship. Edgar Alan Poe's "The Man that was Used Up" and a "dirty" story collected by Gershon Legman[9] also deal with removable bodily parts.

The two stories suggest a confirmation of Mark Twain's belief that American humor had its origin in British humor and that it was the American storyteller's role to Americanize and localize the stories he told, making the humor American rather than British.

Of the stories collected in this anthology, few had yet gone through the process of Americanization. Many are set in England or in other parts of the Old World. Many deal with recognizable British or Old World characters such as Foote. Many tell of recognizable British or Old World buildings or geographical features. Like the Foote anecdote, many of them would reappear with American settings, American characters and American geographical features and buildings. These facts strongly imply that early American almanacs provided a conduit or pipeline between the large reservoir of Old World humor already in existence and the popular consciousness of the American people, but that the American people were unsatisfied with jokes about English people and places. They had to find their own characters to apply the stories to.

Early almanac humor achieves its importance for another reason. It provides us with some conception of what early citizens of the United States considered funny. In turn, that conception reveals much concerning the attitudes of early Americans toward women and the relations between the sexes, about their attitudes toward immigrants and minorities, about their attitudes toward the original possessors of the land, toward lawyers, clergymen, physicians and politicians, about what they considered legitimate business "tricks" and what went beyond the boundaries of legitimacy and about who were their heroes, both comic and serious.

The present collection is a selection of comic items from almanacs published between 1776 and 1800. The selections are from the English language almanacs listed in Charles Evans' *American Bibliography* and reprinted in Gordon K. Shipton's *Early American Imprints, 1639-1800.*[10] I have assumed that these sources provide a sufficient and representative quantity of comic items. The selection has been made according to several criteria. First, repetition has been avoided. Although many of the stories appeared in several almanacs only one example of any story has been given. In the case of similar stories, many were left out in order to avoid repetition. Early almanac makers, for example, seem to have loved examples of Irish "bulls." I have omitted more than half of the "bulls." Most readers will find a sufficient quantity of "bulls" remains.

Second, I have tried to include all of the funniest comic items. An appreciation of humor, as we all know, is highly personal; most readers, however, will find much to laugh at in this anthology.

Third, I have tried to include most of the comic items which had already appeared in an American form. Readers should be aware that "Americanized" jokes do not appear in as high a proportion in the original sources. Their importance justifies their inclusion.

Fourth, whenever I have recognized a comic item that has an analogue in literary or traditional American humor, I have included it. Such items are obviously the most useful for students and scholars of American humor.

Finally, I have tried to include a representative sampling of the subjects of the almanac humor of the early republic. The sampling is not always proportionate, but it is representative of the kinds of subjects found in the almanac humor.

Each of the comic items appears exactly as it appeared in the almanac it was taken from, except that I have modernized and regularized quotation marks and I have used square brackets to indicate words or phrases that are illegible. Sometimes I have indicated what I believe the original word or phrase to have been, but, at other times, it has been impossible even to speculate.

Chapter One
Comic American Heroes

Although many almanac makers were content to reprint British and other Old World comic items, some apparently believed that localized humor was more meaningful and more effective for their purpose, to increase the sale of their almanacs. Such almanac makers were among the leaders in the search for a comic American hero.

The Revolutionary War provided many opportunities for the development of such a hero. Many individuals had acted heroically during the war. Could any of them be treated as comic heroes?

George Washington was even then apparently considered too far above the common hero to be considered in a comic light, but some of his subordinate officers, including Israel Putnam, Henry (Light-Horse Harry) Lee, Benjamin Lincoln, Horatio Gates and Ethan Allen, were considered as possible comic heroes, as were various unnamed officers and enlisted soldiers.

The Revolutionary soldier, named or unnamed, officer or enlisted man, provided a good beginning for the development of an American comic hero, but a nation cannot continue to manufacture its comic hero out of the participants in a war that has ended. America continued to search for a national comic hero. Perhaps one would develop out of the materials provided by the anecdotes of war. In the meantime, America had another candidate.

The wit offered another possibility for an American comic hero, and the America of the early republic could boast of one of the most accomplished wits of all time, an individual who had received world-wide recognition, Benjamin Franklin.

During his life, Franklin had become one of the best known and most popular figures in America. Except for George Washington, it is likely that no American was as well known or as influential as Franklin. American almanacs of the early republic referred to Franklin even more often than they referred to Washington. Almanac makers may have considered Franklin as one of them since he had published an almanac of his own, and it was one of the most imitated almanacs of the century. Almanac makers seemed to believe that anything connected with Franklin would increase the sales of their almanacs.

After Franklin's death, the almanac makers began to mythologize him, publishing and republishing tales that indicated his character as an American comic hero. The stories of Franklin's life reveal a hero with a precocious childhood and youth, a manhood filled with special deeds, a wise old age and the final achievement of immortality.

In addition to military heroes and Benjamin Franklin, early America also had access to Old World stereotypical comic heroes. Five of these stereotypes, the trickster, the fool, the servant, the wit and the countryman achieved importance in the development of an early American comic hero. The five stereotypes overlap. The countryman, for example, was often a fool or trickster. The servant was often a fool and was sometimes adept at repartee. The trickster sometimes took care to appear as a fool. The comic stereotypes, the Revolutionary heroes and Benjamin Franklin all provided elements in a conglomerate that contributed to the formation of the first American comic hero. That many of the comic stereotype anecdotes and tales originated in the Old World does not diminish the Americanism of the comic hero who eventually emerged from them. Perhaps the most important ingredient needed to transform this conglomeration of types into a truly American comic hero was a sense of American pride, and almanacs tended to provide that sense. Many dated themselves not only according to "The Year of our Lord," but also according to "The Year of American Independence." Most of them printed the text of the Constitution when it was being considered for ratification, and many of them printed jokes and anecdotes expressive of American pride.

A. Revolutionary Heroes
1. Israel Putnam

Soon after Mr. Putnam removed from Salem to Pomfret, he found himself and his neighbors infested with wolves which destroyed their sheep. To rid themselves of these ravenous beasts, they resolved to hunt for them, and especially for the ravenous old She wolf which did the most mischief. This wolf had lost the toes of one foot, and thus her tracks were easily known from other's tracks. By this means they pursued her to Connecticut river; then back to Pomfret, where she ran into a cavern or den among the rocks, Mr. Putnam tried to smoke out the wolf by burning straw and brimstone at the mouth of the cave; but without success. He sent in his dogs to worry and drive out the wolf, but the dogs being bitten by the wolf, came out, and would not return. Mr. Putnam then urged a servant to enter the den and shoot the wolf, but he would not venture his life. At length Mr. Putnam determined to risk his own life, and if possible, kill the wolf. The cavern was so small that he was obliged to creep on his belly. He therefore took a strip of birch bark, and lighted it, and having a rope tied to one leg, by which he might be pulled out, when he should give the signal, he crept into the den. When he had come near the wolf, she gnashed her teeth and began to growl. He saw the glaring eyeballs of the wolf and kicking the rope, he was [pulled] out of the den so suddenly as to be stripped of his cloaths.

Having loaded his gun with buckshot, he entered a second time, and as he approached the wolf, she growled, [   ] led her eyes, and snapped her teeth. Observing this, Mr. Putnam levelled his musket and fired; instantly he was drawn out, half suffocated with smoke and stunned with the noise. As soon as the den was cleared of smoke, he entered a third time, and putting the torch to the wolf's nose, found she was dead. Then taking her by the ears, he kicked the rope, and his friends drew him and the wolf out together.

Such is the effect of courage! Everyone who wishes to be a hero, must be as bold as the brave Putnam.[1]

During the French war, when General Amherst commanded the British troops in America, and when he was marching across the country to Canada, the army coming to one of the lakes which they were obliged to pass, found the French had an armed vessel of 12 guns upon it. He was in great distress, his boats were no match for her; and she alone was capable of sinking his whole army in that situation. While he was pondering what should be done, Putnam came to him and said, " *General, that ship must be taken.*" "Aye," says Amherst, "I would give the world she was taken." "I'll take her," says Putnam. Amherst smiled and asked how? "Give me some wedges, a beetle and a few men of my own choice." Amherst could not conceive of how an armed vessel was to be taken by four or five men, a beetle and wedges. However, he granted Putnam's request. When night came, Putnam, with his materials and men, went in a boat under the vessel's stern, and in an instant drove in the wedges behind the rudder, in the little cavity between the rudder and the ship, and left her. In the morning the sails were seen fluttering about, she was adrift in the middle of the lake; and being presently blown ashore, she was easily taken. (*Carleton's Almanack...for...1793* (24177))

A person by the name of Palmer, who was a lieutenant in the tory new levie, was detected in the camp at Peeks Kill. Governor Tryon, who commanded the new levies, reclaimed him as a British officer, represented the heinous crime of condemning a man commissioned by his Majesty, and threatened vengeance in case he should be executed. General Putnam wrote him the following pithy reply.

"Sir,

Nathan Palmer, a Lieutenant in your King's service, was taken in my camp as a *spy*—he was tried as a *spy*—he was condemned as a *spy*—and you may rest assured, Sir, he shall be hanged as a *spy*. I have the honour to be, &c.

Israel Putnam

P.S. Afternoon—he is hanged."
(*Greenleaf's New-York, Connecticut and New Hampshire Almanack-*... *for*...*1791* (22332))

2. General Lee

General Lee being one day surrounded, according to custom, by a numerous levee of his canine favourites, was asked by a lady if he liked dogs? With his usual politeness, he instantly replied, "Yes madam; I love dogs; but I detest bitches." (*Father Hutchin's Revived*...*for*...*1793* (24416))

During the time of the attack on Sullivan Island General Lee was one day reconnoitering communication made by the bridge of boats [between] that place and the continent. As the balls whi [rled] about in abundance, he observed one of his aide-de-camps, a very young man, shrink every now and then, and by the motion of his body, wished to avoid if possibly, the shot,
" 'S[blood], Sir," cried he, "what do you mean? Do you dodge? Do you know the king of Prussia lost above an hundred aid-de-camps in one campaign?" "So I understand, Sir," replied [the] young officer, "but I did not think you could sp[are] so many." (*Keatinge's Maryland Almanack for*...*1800* (35151))

3. Other generals and officers

The late Col. Ethan Allen had a high opinion of himself and his six brothers, and took occasion to observe that there were *never* seven such born of any woman. "You are mistaken," said a Scotch officer, "*Mary Magdelen* was delivered of *seven exactly like you.*" (*Beers's Almanac-*...*for*...*1793*(24083))

When the gallant general Wayne received his wound in storming the forts at Stony-Point he was a good deal staggered, and fell upon one knee; but the moment he recovered himself, he called to his aide who supported him, and said, "lead me forward: if I am mortally wounded, let me die in the fort." (*The Virginia Almanack, for*...*1796*(28197))

The following anecdote will explain the meaning of the title given to general Gates, *of Burgoyne's midwife.*

Soon after the capture of general Burgoyne at Saratoga, he was in company with general Gates, his aged captor. In consequence of the free circulation of the bottle, the prisoner forgot his captivity, and gave way to his wit. The conversation turning to the plains of Saratoga, the British general reproached Gates for undertaking the command of an army at a period of life when declining years admonished him to undertake the office of midwife rather than a general. "A midwife!" exclaimed the veteran, "You know from experience, that in discharging the duties of a general, I did not forget the office of midwife, for in one day I safely delivered you of 7,000 soldiers, with whom you had been long in labour." (*Father Abraham's Almanac, for... 1798*(32310))

In the American war, two brothers were Colonel and Lieutenant Colonel of the same regiment. A shot brought down the Colonel's horse— "One inch more," (said the younger brother), "and I should have commanded the regiment." (*Carleton's Almanack ... for... 1794*(25261))

4. A simple soldier

At the battle of Danbury, a New-England soldier seated himself upon a fence, within gunshot of the British, and from thence fired thirty-two charges at them, without being touched by a single one of the bullets aimed at him. When he found his ammunition spent, he dismounted in haste, and holding up his open cartridge-box to shew its emptiness, he precipitately fled, repeating aloud as he ran these very pertinent lines:—

> He that fights and runs away,
> May live to fight another day
> But he that is in the battle slain
> Shall never live to fight again.

(*The Wilmington Almanac...for...1794* (25494))

During the late war when draughts were made from the militia, to recruit the continental army, a certain captain gave liberty to the men who were draughted from his company to make their objections if they had any, against going into the service. Accordingly, one of them, who had an impediment in his speech, came up to the captain. "I ca-a-ant go because I stutter." "Stutter!" says the captain, "you don't go there to talk, but to fight." "Aye, but they'll p-p-put me upon g-g-guard, and a man may get ha-half a mile, before I can say wh-wh-who goes there!" "Oh that is no objection, for they will place some other sentry with you, and he can challenge if you can fire." "Well, b-b-but I may be ta-ta-taken and run through the g-g-guts, before I can cry qu-qu-quarter." This last prevailed, and the captain out of humanity, (laughed heartily) and dismissed him. (*The Wilmington Almanac...for...1794* (25494))

B. Benjamin Franklin

Dr. Franklin, when a child, found the long graces of his father before and after meals very disagreeable. One day, after the winter's provisions had been salted, "I think, father," says Benjamin, "if you said *grace* over the *whole task*—once for all—it would be a vast *saving of time.*" (*The Wilmington Almanack... for...1792*(23383))

Doctor Franklin, at age ten, played leap frog, but fell heels over head. A companion cried out, "Ben, you are as lively as a bee!"—"Yes," replied Ben, "but not a Honey Bee nor a Bumble-Bee, but a careless Boobe." (*Webster's Calendar; or the Albany Almanack, for...1797* (31617))

The late Dr. Franklin, in the early part of his life followed the business of a printer, and had occasion to travel from Philadelphia to Boston. In his journey, he stopped at one of their inns, the landlord of which possessed the true disposition of his countrymen, which is to be inquisitive, even to impertinence, into the business of every stranger. The Doctor, after the fatigue of the day's travel, had set himself down to supper, when his landlord began to torment him with questions. The Doctor well knew the disposition of those people and apprehended, that, after having answered his questions others would come in and go over the same ground, and he determined to stop him. "Have you a wife landlord?" "Yes, Sir." "Pray let me see her." Madam was introduced with much form. "How many children have you?" "Four, Sir." "I should be happy to see them." The children were sought and introduced. "How many servants have you?" "Two Sir, a man and a woman." "Pray fetch them." When they came, the Doctor asked if there were any other persons in the house, and being answered in the negative addressed them with much solemnity. "My good friends I sent for you here to give an account of myself. My name is BENJAMIN FRANKLIN. I am a printer, of ____ years of age, reside at Philadelphia and am going from thence to Boston. I sent for you all, that, if you wish for any further particulars, you may ask, and I will inform you, which done, *I flatter myself, you will permit me to eat my supper in peace.*" (*Weatherwise's Almanack, for 1797* (31583))

Dr. Franklin, as Agent for the province of Pennsylvania, being in England, at the time the Parliament passed the Stamp-Act for America, was frequently applied to by the Ministry, for his opinion respecting the same, and he assured them, that the People of America would never submit to it. The Act was nevertheless passed; and the event shewd he had been right. After the news of the destruction of the stamped paper had arrived in England, the Ministry again sent for the Doctor to consult with him, and concluded with this position; that, if the Americans would engage to pay for the damage done in the destruction of the paper, &c. the Parliament would repeal the Act. To this, the Doctor answered that it put him in mind of a Frenchman who heated a poker red hot, ran into the street and addressed an Englishman he met there, "Hah, Monsieur, voulez vous give me de plaisir et de satisfaction and lete me runi dis poker one foote up your backside?:' "What!" said the Englishman. "Only to lete me runi dis poker one foote up your backside." "Hang your head!" replied the Englishman. "Welle, den, only so far," said the Frenchman, pointing to about six inches of the poker. "No, no," replied the Englishman—"Hang your body: What do you mean?" "Well, den," said the Frenchman, "will you have de justice to paye me for de trouble and expence of heating the poker?" "No, damn if I do," answered the Englishman; and walked off. (*Wait's York, Cumberland and Lincoln Almanack, for... 1794* (25733))

Anecdote of the late Dr. Franklin

Being in company with a Reverend gentleman who was expatiating largely on the importance of a uniformity in religious worship; the Doctor told him he could find something in the Bible which seemed opposed to his opinion; and reaching down one from a shelf opened it and read as follows:—

"And it came to pass after these things, that Abraham sat in the door of his tent, about the going down of the sun, and behold, a man, bent with age, coming from the way of the wilderness, leaning on a staff. And Abraham arose, and met him and said unto him, 'turn in, I pray thee, and wash thy feet; and tarry all night; and thou shalt arise early in the morning and go thy way.' And the man said, 'nay; for I will abide under this tree.' But Abraham pressed him greatly: so he turned and they went into the tent: and Abraham baked unleavened bread, and they did eat. And when Abraham saw that the man blessed not God, he said unto him, 'wherefore dost thou not worship the most high God, Creator of heaven and earth?' And the man answered and said, 'I do not worship thy God, neither do I call upon his name; for I have made to myself a God, which abideth always in my house, and provideth me with all things.' And Abraham's zeal was kindled against the man, and he arose and fell upon him, and drove him forth with blows into the wilderness. And God called unto Abraham, saying 'Abraham, where is the stranger?' And Abraham answered and said, 'Lord, he would not worship thee, neither would he call upon thy name; therefore I have driven him out from before my face into the wilderness.' And God said, 'have I borne with him these hundred and ninety years, and nourished him, and clothed him, notwithstanding his rebellion against me; and could not thou, who art thyself a sinner, bear with him one night.' "

After he had gone through, the Divine expressed great surprize that he should have forgot this account and enquired what Chapter contained it. The Doctor referred him to the 27th Chapter of Genesis. The fact was, the whole was an ingenious device of the learned Doctor, to impress the duty of religious toleration on his antagonist. (*The Federal Almanack for. . . 1795* (28065))

Dr. Franklin, wishing to amuse himself with the credulity of the votaries of Philosophy proposed to the Royal Society of London the following question, of which he requested a solution, viz. "Why will a tub, with a fish in it, contain as much water as it will without a fish."

Many academical Pates were employed in solving this difficult problem. Many ingenious solutions were delivered in, but, just as they were proceeding to publish the one which was deemed the most so, the Doctor informed them that there was a small inaccuracy in their operations which he begged leave to rectify, by assuring them, That a tub with a fish in it would *not* contain as much water, as if the fish were out. (*The Columbian Almanac for. . . 1796* (28450))

The late Sir John Pringle, in travelling through France, with Dr. Franklin, had a very violent dispute with him, respecting the manner in which the complaint called catching cold is produced: one of them persisting, that it arose from repletion, the other from application of cold air to the body. They agreed, therefore, each to make an experiment on himself. The one, not used to suppers, ate an extremely hearty one. The other sat up a great part of the night near an open window. Neither of them was, however, able to maintain his own theory of the disorder by the experiment, for neither of them caught cold. (*Father Abraham's Alamanac for. . . 1794* (25579))

At the conclusion of the American war, Dr. Franklin, the English ambassador, and the French minister Vergennes, dining together at Versailles, a toast from each was called for and agreed to—The British minister began his with "George the third, who like the sun in its meridian, spreads a lustre throughout and enlightens the world." The French minister followed with "The illustrious Louis the Sixteenth, who, like the moon, sheds his mild and benignant rays on, and influences the globe." Our American,

Franklin, then gave "George Washington, Commander in Chief of the American Armies, who, like Joshua of old, commanded the Sun and the Moon to stand still, and they obeyed him." (*The Farmer's Almanack- ...for...1798* (32921))

Dr. Price once asked the question, "Why our eyes failed us in old age, when we needed them most?" Dr. Franklin replied, "that dimness of sight in old men was attended with this advantage, that they could not see the wrinkles in their wives faces." (*Bickerstaff's Connecticut Almanack, for...'1791*(23068))

Dr. Franklin, when last in England, used pleasantly to repeat an observation of his negro servant, when the Doctor was making the tour of Derbyshire, Lancashire, etc. "Everything, Massa, work in this country, water work; wind work; fire work, smoke work; dog work; (he had before noticed the last at Bath) man work; bullock work; horse work; ass work; every thing work here but de hog! he eat, he drink, he sleep, he do nothing all day; the hog be the only gentleman in England." (*The Citizen and Farmer's Almanac, for...1801* (37185))

Anecdote of Dr. Franklin
While he was President of the State of Pennsylvania, the Doans, it may be remembered, were tried, condemned and executed.—A religious madman called upon the President, and asserted that he was sent to command him to grant a reprieve to those unfortunate young men.—"Who sent you?"— "The Lord."—"You are an imposter," replied Dr. Franklin—"The Lord could not have sent you on so silly an errand; *they were hanged two hours ago.*" (*Beers's Almanac...for...1793* (24083)

An ODE on the late Dr. Benjamin Franklin

> Hark! hear the solemn sound!
> Which strikes with awe profound!
>   Columbia's sons.
> Franklin the great is dead,
> To happier regions fled
> Where laurels grace his head,
>   And shining crowns.
> The electric fluid brought,
> By thee, such wonders wrought,
>   Thou matchless sage.
> The lightning's livid glare,
> You taught us not to fear,

But did repellents rear,
To stop its rage.
How much to him we ow'd.
Such services bestow'd
By Franklin's pen
A treaty made with France,
Our glorious cause advanc'd
Whilst Gallia's sons made grants,
Freed us again.
Columbia's Genii mourn
Her statesman now is gone,
To worlds on high.
His works on earth shall shine,
Wisdom almost divine,
Deep thought with worth combin'd
That struck the sky.
In cypress' solemn shades,
Where sorrow e'er pervades,
That gloomy grove
Shall Freedom's sons repair
And drop the silent tear,
Prevailing with despair,
Their fondest love.
Accept blest shade the sigh,
Piercing with agony,
Our tender hearts:
Your name is deep impress'd
On every Frenchman's breast;
Your soul in heaven is blest
For thy efforts.
Heaven claimed thee for her own
To sit on shining throne
With matchless grace.
Where Freedom's guardian God,
Thy glorious deeds applaud,
And spread thy fame abroad,
Through every place.

(*Weatherwise's Town and Country Almanack, for... 1792*(23964))

C. Stock Stereotypes
   1. Fools

Giles Jolt and his cart.
Giles Jolt, as sleeping in his cart he lay,
Some pilf'ring villain stole his team away:
Giles wakes, and cries—"What's here, a dickins, what!
Why how now—am I Giles, or am I not?
If he—I've lost six geldings to my smart:
If not' oddsbuddikins, I've found a cart."
(*Loudon's Almanack...for...1786* (19499))

A very small gentleman challenged a very large man to a duel; "I have," says the large man, "a very unequal chance on account of your diminutive size; I will chalk out a picture of you on my belly, and if you shoot outside of the mark, why, *it shan't go, and you shall fire again.*" (*An Astronomical Diary, or Almanack, for...1796* (29493))

As the commissioners were lately running anew, the line between North and South Carolina, it chanced to carry a certain house into North Carolina, which according to the old line, stood a rod over on the other state. The good old woman who lived in the house, upon being ascertained of the transaction, exclaimed—"Now we have got into the other state, and I'm dear glad on't, for I always heard that South Carolina was a *desperate unhealthy place.*" (*The Farmer's Almanack, for...1799* (34968))

One came to visit a gentleman in the country, and finding him eating some cherries with his spectacles on, having asked his reason for it, he answered, " *The truth is, I bade my man bring me Kentish cherries, and the knave has brought me these little ones which you see; therefore I eat them with my spectacles on to make them look bigger.*" (*Beers's Alamanac for...1800* (35164))

A certain Paddy, newly transported into this country, passed by where a farmer was gathering pumpkins. "By my should and what do you call them," said Paddy—"Mares eggs," says the farmer. "And by St. Patrick, and won't you sell me one of them? for I wish to get in the way of raising my own horses, for my poor old father straightened the hemp for nothing but taking one without liberty"—"Yes, yes, for a quarter of a dollar you may take one." So Paddy takes it and on he goes—and in descending the hill he by chance let the pumpkin fall, and it took a direction down the hill toward a bunch of bushes, and Mr. Paddy in full speed after it. The pumpkin struck a stump and split open—a rabbit which lay under the bush asleep started, almost frightened to death, and Paddy after it yelling—"Stop that coult! stop that coult! stop that coult!" (*The Connecticut Pocket Almanac, for... 1800* (36384))

2. Countrymen

A clown in Berkshire employed to draw timber, from a wood, met with an oak trunk of so large a size that the tackle he made use of to place it on the carriage broke twice in the trial. Hodge flung his hat on the ground, and scratching his head with much vexation, exclaimed, "Damn the hogs that didn't eat thee when thee was an acorn, and then I shouldn't have had this trouble with thee." (*The Virginia Almanack, for... 1788* (20199))

A peasant being at confession accused himself of having stolen some hay—The father confessor asked him how many bundles he had taken from the stack?—"That is of no consequence," said the peasant, "you may set it down a waggon load, for my wife and I are to go and fetch the remainder very soon." (*Barber's Albany Almanack, for... 1789* (21178))

A merchant having trusted a Countryman with a number of articles, made out his account and sent it to him. In it were articles which he had taken up at different times, and instead of naming the articles every time he put *Ditto*. The countryman not understanding the word asked some young fellows what it meant, they told him it was some sort of cloth. The countryman went to the merchant in a rage, and inquired why he charged him with ditto, declaring he never had any such article! The merchant explained it to him and he was satisfied; Upon his return the young fellows asked him if he had found out the merchant's meaning. "Yes," replied the countryman, "I found out that I was an intollerable fool, and you were Ditto." (*The Universal Calendar, and the North American Almanack, for... 1789* (21476))

A few days ago a lady in the Fly-Market, (New York) took off her glove to take up some fruit, to look at, the countrywoman asked the reason of her hand being so white? The lady replied, "it was because she wore dog skin gloves!" " *Bless me,*" cried the old woman: " *my husband has wore dog skin small clothes these three years, and his ————— is as brown as a nutmeg.*" (*Ames's Almanack, for... 1792* (23121))

A farmer in Londonderry (New Hampshire) having occassion to make some new yokes, and having no auger suitable to bore them sent a lad with message requesting to borrow an auger who sternly replied, "I'll not lend my auger—tell your father he may bring his yokes here, and bore them."—Soon after, this neighbour had occassion to borrow a plough, and sent to the farmer requesting the loan of his, who in his turn, replied, "I'll not lend my plough—he may bring his land here and plough it." (*Carleton's Almanack...for... 1794* (25261))

A Lady of Equestrian fame, riding full speed was thrown from her horse by an unexpected stumble, with such violence, that she rolled over once or twice, something in the stile of a Derbyshire exhibition. On getting up, she saw her footman, who was riding behind her, laughing to himself, and was resolved to know, as he was a kind of country bumpkin, whether she had fallen decently or not?—"Pray, John," said the Lady, "Did you see my agility." "Whoi, to be sure madam, I can't say but what I did, but I never heard IT called so afore." (*The Kentucky Almanac, for...1794* (25688))

A country clergyman, a short time since, was abruptly called upon by a rustick, who very earnestly entreated him to accompany him immediately to christen a *few* new-born children. "A few" (replied the clergyman) "don't you know how many of them there are?"—"Not rightly," says the fellow, scratching his head; "there were but three of them when I came out; but the Lord knows how many there are by this time!" (*Stoddard's Diary: or, the Columbia Almanack, for... 1798* (31788))

Some years since, a sober, zealous, Connecticut parson went to catechize a family in his parish, who were not as well versed in the rudiments of divinity as many are: when he arrived he thought proper to begin with Lois, the eldest daughter, a girl about eighteen, and buxom as May whose charms had smitten the young village swains with an epidemic. "Well Lois," said the parson, "I shall begin with you—come tell me who died for you?" Lois with a charming flush on her cheeks replied—"Why nobody as I know *on.*" The parson, rather surprised at her answer, repeated his question with increasing zeal—"Lois, I say tell me who died for you." Poor Lois, rather irritated at the inquisitive parson, again replied, "Why *nobody*, sir—there was Tom Dawton lay bed rid for me about six months, but folks *says* he got about again." (*The American Almanac, for... 1798* (31836))

An aged woman living in the back parts of Pennsylvania, several miles from the church, went one Sunday merely out of curiosity to see the priest. As she entered the church, he was relating the sufferings and death of our blessed Saviour.—She, desirous of being informed, asked him when it happened, said she never heard of it before, for it had been forty years since their folks had taken the newspaper. (*The New-England Almanac...for... 1798* (32012))

A gentlemen of this vicinity, being on a journey to the eastward, had rode but a few miles before he was seized with such a violent cholic that he was obliged to alight at a small cottage by the road-side to procure some relief. The mistress of the dwelling, who was a *motherly old woman,* immediately recommended swallowing a bullet; observing at the same time, that she had done it a *power of times*, and it was always sure to ease the pain. The gentleman, being in agony, was willing to receive anything that came in the shape of advice; therefore, accepting a bullet from the hands of his sagacious *doctress*, swallowed it, and proceeded on his journey. He found immediate relief; and on his return called to thank the old lady for her kind attention.—"Ah!" said she, in reply, " *I knew 'twould cure you, for I have swallowed the same bullet eleven times myself, and never knew it fail."* (*Stoddard's Diary: or, the Columbia Almanack, for... 1799* (33391))

A plain country yeoman bringing his daughter to town, said, for all she was brought up altogether in the country, she was a girl of sense. *"Yes,"* says a pretty young female in the company, *"country sense."* "Why, faith, Madam," says the honest yeoman, *"'country sense is better some times, than town impudence."* (*The Kentucky Almanack...for...1799* (33954))

A countryman being requested to help a member of Congress out of a ditch, replied that he had no hand in *state affairs.* *(Isaiah Thomas's Massachusetts, Connecticut, Rhodeisland, Newhampshire, and Vermont Almanack...for...1799* (34652))

A countryman sowing his ground, two smart fellows riding that way, one of them called to him with an insolent air; "well, honest fellow, it is your business to sow, but we shall reap the fruits of your labor." To which the countryman replied, " 'Tis very likely, for I am sowing hemp." (*The Farmer's Almanac, for... 1800* (35167))

An honest country farmer meeting the parson of the parish in a narrow lane, and not giving him the way so readily as he expected, the parson, in a haughty tone, told him—he was better fed than taught; "very true indeed, Sir," replied the farmer, "for you teach me, and I feed myself." (*The Farmer's Almanack...for...1800* (36414))

A countryman, seeing a lady in the street, in a very odd dress as he thought, says to her, "Madam, if I may be so bold, what do you call this?" taking hold of the dress. The lady, not a little surprised at the question called him an impertinent fellow. "Nay, I hope no offence," cried *Jonathan,* "I am a poor countryman, just going out of town, and my woman always expects I should bring her an account of the newest fashions which occasioned my asking what you call this thing that you wear." "It is a sack," said the lady in a pet. "I vow," (replied the countryman, heartily nettled at her behaviour) *"I have heard of a pig in a poke, but I'll swamp it, if ever I saw a sow in a sack before.*" (*The Columbia Alamanac: or, the North American Calendar for... 1801* (37206))

3. Tricksters

An Astrologer in the Reign of Louis the 11th of France, having foretold something disagreeable to the King, the King in Revenge, was resolved to have him killed. The next Day he sent for the Astrologer and ordered the People about him, at a Signal given, to throw the Astrologer out of the Window. As soon as the King saw him, "You that pretend," (says he) "to be such a wise man, and know so perfectly the fate of others, inform me a little what will be your own, and how long you are to live." The Astrologer, who now began to apprehend some danger, answered with great Presence of Mind, "I know my Destiny, and am certain I shall die three Days before your Majesty." The King, on this, was so far from having him thrown out of the Window that, on the contrary, he took a particular care not to suffer him to want any Thing, and did all that was possible to retard the Death of a Man which his own was so closely to follow. (*The Wilmington Almanack...for...1782* (17157))

Two traders were proceeding on a pilgrimage. A countryman, who was prosecuting the same journey, having joined them on the road, they agreed to travel together, and make a joint stock of their provisions. But when arrived within a day's journey of the holy place, it was almost wholly expended, so that they had nothing left but a little flour barely sufficient to make a small cake. The perfidious traders entered into a plot together, to cheat their companion of his share, and from his stupid air, imagined they could dupe him without difficulty. "We must come to some agreement," said one of the citizens, "What will not assuage the hunger of three, may satisfy a single person, and I vote that it be alotted to one of us only. But that each may have a fair chance, I propose that we all three lie down and fall asleep, and that the bread may be the lot of him, who, on waking, shall have had the most curious dream."

The other citizen, as we may readily suppose, approved vastly this suggestion. The countryman also signified his approbation, and pretended to give completely into the snare. They then made the bread, put it on the fire to bake, and lay down. But our tradesmen were so fatigued with their journey, that without intending it they fell soon into a profound slumber. The clown, more cunning, waited only this opportunity; got up without noise, went and ate the bread, and then composed himself to rest.

Soon after one of the citizens awaked, and calling to his companions, "Friends," said he, "listen to my dream. I thought myself transported by two angels into hell. For a long time they kept me suspended over the abyss

of everlasting fire. There I was a witness to the torments of the damned."
"And I," said the other, "dreamed that the gates of Heaven were opened
to me. The arch-angels, Michael and Gabriel, after raising me up into the
sky, carried me before the throne of God. There I was a spectator of his
glory." And then the dreamer began to recount the wonders of Paradise,
as the other had of the infernal abodes.

The Countryman, meanwhile, though he heard perfectly well what
they had said, pretended to be still asleep. They went to rouse him from
his slumbers; when he affecting the surprize of a man suddenly disturbed
from his rest, cried out, "What's the matter?" "Why it is only your fellow
travellers. What! do you not recollect us? Come rise and inform us of your
dream."

"My dream? O, I have had a very droll one, and one that I am
sure will afford you some diversion. When I saw you both carried away,
the one to Heaven the other to Hell; I thought that I had lost you forever.
I then got up, and as I never expected to see you more, I went and demolished
the loaf." (*Loudon's Almanack...for...1787* (19500))

A felon in travelling was Moneyless and hungry, wherefore to supply
his belly he set his wits to work: coming by a knight's house about dinner
time, he knocks at the gate, and enquires for the Steward, who coming
to him, he asks him if his master would buy a wedge of gold of a foot
and half long? The Steward imagining he had such a one about him to
sell, invites him in and tells his master of it. The Knight, hearing of such
a prize bids his Steward to make much of him and feast him with the best.
After dinner the Knight sent for him into his Parlour, and asked him if
he would speak with him? "Yes," said the fellow, "I come to know if you
would buy a wedge of gold of a foot and a half long." The Knight told
him, "Yes," he cared not if he did. "Then," said the fellow, "now that
I know your mind, if I should find one of that length, I will bring it to
you." (*Bickerstaff's New-England Almanack, for... 1787* (20137))

A person went lately to a storekeeper's and offered to sell him some
hardware assuring him he could sell cheaper than any man because he was
the maker. The goods were purchased. Next day another came with the
same kind of hardware, and told the storekeeper he could sell cheaper than
any man because he had them from the maker. "I bought," replied the
storekeeper, "from the maker yesterday: can you sell cheaper than him?"
*"O yes, sir, I don't intend to pay him." (Father Tammany's Almanac,
for...1787* (20160))

The Countess of Jervac, having some time since lost a favorite lap-dog, desired a friend, on his next passing over the Pont-neuf, to replace it, by purchasing another from the people, who there vend these animals. The gentleman, accordingly bought for two Louis, the handsomest in the place. The Countess became instantly enamoured of the beauty of its colour, and the silkness of its coat. The new favourite was the admiration of every visitant, until one gentleman unfortunately observed that it had a little stiffness in its walk. The dear creature was taken up to examine into the cause of its lameness, when a seam presented itself running along the belly, which being rip't and pursued with great caution, out skipped a little black mongrel puppy. The Countess was astonished—the visitors stared—but the little animal himself, seemed greatly rejoiced at being released from the skin into which he had been inserted with so much ingenuity. (*Wheeler's North American Calendar...for...1789* (21597))

A strange gentleman being much necessitated for a house of office in the city, and being unacquainted went into an upholsterers shop, and bid him shew him a close stool. When he shewed him one, "What?" said he "have you no better?" "Yes," says he, "all of covered velvet." "Go," says he, "fetch me two or three down," in the meantime he placed himself down in one: The upholsterer coming down and seeing him in that posture, asked him what he was doing? "Why, truly," says he, "I am trying of it; but they are all too low for me," and so went off. (*The Federal Almanack, for...1791* (23043))

Three or four roguish scholars walking out one day from the University of Oxford, spied a poor fellow near Abington, asleep in a ditch, with an ass by him, loaded with earthen ware, holding the bridle in his hand, says one of the scholars to the rest, "if you'll assist me, I'll help you to a little money, for you know we are bare at present:" No doubt of it they were not long in consenting; "Why then," said he, "we'll go and sell this old fellow's ass at Abington, for you know the fair is tomorrow, and we shall meet with chapmen enough; therefore, do you take the panniers off, put them on my back, and that bridle over my head, then lead the ass to market and let me alone with the old man." This being done accordingly in a little time after the poor man awaking, was strangely surprised to see his ass thus metamorphosed: "O! for God's sake," said the scholar, "take this bridle out of my mouth and this load from my back." "Zouns, how come you here?" replied the old man. "Why," said he, "my father who is a necromancer, upon an idle thing I did to disoblige him, transformed me into an ass; but now his heart was relented, and I am come into my own shape again, I beg you will let me go home and thank him!" "By all means," said the crockery merchant, "I don't desire to have any thing to do with conjuration," and so set the scholar at liberty, who went directly to his comrades, that by this time were making merry with the money they had sold the ass for: But the old fellow was forced to go next day to seek for a new one in the fair, and after having look'd on several, his own was shewn him for a very good one: "O, ho," said he, "what has he and his father quarreled again? No, no, I'd have nothing to say to him." (*Father Abraham's Almanac, for . . .1793* (24311))

A brisk young sempstress having outwitted many an airy fop and sparkish gallant, was at last outwitted herself in the following manner: a town shift, in a very good habit, coming into her shop, [   ] bargained for a considerable parcel of linen; and then pausing—said, "Oh, I'd like to forgot one thing: I want a shirt of the largest make: It is not for myself, but for one as big again." She shewed him thereupon several; but he complained they were too straight; and she then shewed another; which he seemed to like, saying, "Pray madam, do me the favour to slip it over your own clothes;" which to please and humour so good a customer, she did. Then he turned her about to see how it sat, fastened privately the hinder lappets with two large pins, through all her clothes into the hinder parts of her smock; then snatching the linen he had bargained for off the counter, out he ran;—she thereupon followed him, crying, "Stop him! stop him! and hastily going to pull the shirt over her ears, as ashamed to pursue him in such a garment, she with it drew up all her clothes and exposed her naked posteriors to the publick; and so ran on, still pulling to get off the shirt; whilst some matrons, who supposed her to be mad, stopped her, sensible that she ought to be covered behind; which gave the sharper an opportunity to run cleverly off with his booty. (*The Wilmington Almanac . . .for . . .1794* (25494))

The celebrated Burroughs, visiting a clergyman where he was not known, engaged to preach for him; but previous to Sunday morning, decamped with his brother's cash; and left the following words, for the morrow's text, " *Ye shall seek me, and shall not find me.*" (*Beers's Almanac . . .for . . .1795* (26632))

A Remarkable Imposition
The following imposition was absolutely practiced upon a taylor and salesman in a certain town some time ago. A person of genteel appearance coming to the shop, requested if a suit of cloaths could be made in a few days, as he was under the necessity of going to Scotland at the expiration of that period: being answered in the affirmative, he was measured accordingly. Having a painting with him that he said was of such value that a gentleman at Edinburgh had offered him eighty guineas for it, he

desired to leave the same with the taylor till his cloathes were finished, assigning for his reason, that, having discharged his lodgings he should remain with a slight acquaintance at the other end of town, 'till his cloaths &c. were ready for his departure. This being readily acceded to, the picture was hung up by the taylor in a parlour contiguous to the shop. On the next day a gentleman in appearance, but in reality a person procured by the former, coming into the shop and purchasing a trivial article, pretended the utmost astonishment at seeing the painting, enquiring where the salesman got it, whether it was to be sold, &c. &c. On being told it belonged to a gentleman who had been offered eighty guineas for it, he offered to purchase it for a hundred, counting them out of his purse at the same time; and being told that the gentleman's consent could not be immediately obtained, he proposed calling again in a few days for an answer. In the interval the former person that bespoke the cloaths, calling for them according to appointment, was informed (the taylor thinking to avail himself of the other's partiality for the picture) that a gentleman accidentally seeing it had offered eighty guineas for it, adding, that as it would save the trouble of carriage, he would, to prevent the gentleman's hindrance, purchase it for the former, having received from him his address, said to be in a square near Oxford Street, &c. With some seeming reluctance this was at last agreed to. The taylor, deducting for the cloaths, paid the money; the other decamping, left him in vain to search for the amateur in painting—and the picture being shewn to an artist, proved to be worth about forty shillings. (*The Monmouth Almanac, for... 1795*(27018))

Two very honest gentlemen who sold brooms meeting one day in the street, one asked the other, How the devil he could afford to under sell him every where as he did, when he *stole* the stuff, and made the brooms himself? "Why, you silly dog," answered the other, " *I steal them ready made.*" (*The Farmer's Almanack... for...1796*(29626))

Mr. C____n of Clagwell in Essex, sent a [fine] hare to his friend in London: the man by whom it was sent having stopped at an alehouse near Stratford, called for a pint of beer, and went backwards; in the meantime, the landlord cruelly killed his cat, and put it into the basket in lieu of the hare, which he concealed; the man pursued his journey, sent in the basket; was called in himself, and asked if he had stopped on the road? He answered in the affirmative and the mystery was cleared up. He received a reward with thanks to his master for the intended present. He marched back with the cat, called again at the pot-house, where he found only the servant girl, and a pot boiling; he called for another pint, and sent the girl for a penny-worth of tobacco; in the mean-time, he took a fine piece of beef out of the pot, and put in the cat. And then went off. (*Father Tammany's Almanac, for...1796* (29925))

A wag, some time ago advertised a carriage to perform without horses, with only one wheel, and invited the curious in mechanics to see it. Many of the members of the society of arts attended, and, in the ardor of expectation, where shewn—*a wheelbarrow.* (*The United States Almanac for...1797* (30614))

Knavery is almost always its own punishment, as virtue is its own reward. A woman who had brought some light pounds of butter to market, had the good luck to sell them all but one, before the clerk of the market came about: when she perceived the officer of justice, she began to dread the fate of her last roll; however, iniquity is fertile in expedients, she thought it did not want more than two ounces to make it a pound, and therefore, as the clerk approached, she squeezed two dollars into the roll, to make it the right weight: the clerk came, weighed the butter—it was still too light; he threw it into his basket, dollars and all, and stepped away to inspect the butter of another woman, who, to avoid the possibility of censure or loss, had put it up half an ounce above the standard weight. (*The Town and Country Almanack, for... 1797*(31616))

A scholar, a bald man, and a barber, travelling together, agreed each to watch four hours at night, in turn, for the sake of security. The barber's lot came first, who shaved the scholar's head when asleep, then awaked him when his turn came. The scholar scratching his head, and feeling it bald, exclaimed, "You wretch of a barber, you have waked the bald man instead of me!" (*The Town and Country Almanac, for...1799* (34545))

The noted Sam Foote, an English comedian of facetious memory, and one of the greatest humourists that ever existed, once, during his summer theatrical recess, took into his head to go down into the country with a set of companions, every one of whom had been accidentally deprived of some limb or member of the body, such as one or both arms, a leg, a thigh, &c.—Foote himself, it is well known, had lost one leg; and over the wooden one, that supplied its place, he wore a boot so exactly fitted that the defect could scarcely be discovered by the most curious observer. The company alighted one evening from the stage coach, at a public house, the driver, who had a wooden nose, ordered his horses to be taken care of for the night, as the travellers meant to sup and lie at the inn—this was accordingly done. Supper was ordered, and the company passed the evening with great humour over some choice old Madeira wine. About two in the morning Foote called to the landlord for a bed, and desired the waiter to come and draw off his boots, The fellow in attempting this bit of service, was half frighted out of his wits, when he found that one of the man's legs came off with the boot; and starting back, left Foote to disengage the other himself.—"Sir," (cried another guest to the landlord) "be so kind as to lay by this eye of mine, and be sure to let me have it well cleaned in the morning by the time I get up."—The stage driver then came in, and presented his wooden nose to the landlord, wishing him to lay it in a drawer till morning. The landlord and the waiter both stared but concealed their fears as much as possible, supposing they had got a company of apparitions.—Another of the friends then desiring assistance in pulling off his coat, away came both arms apparently flesh, bone and all, nearly from the shoulders, to the increased astonishment of the affrightened landlord. A guest that had hitherto sat very quietly over his bottle of wine, rousing himself all of a sudden, and rubbing his eyes, called to the master of the house, and requested him "to be so obliging as to lift off his head, and lay it by in the barroom; for faith," (says he), "I am sleepy, and it's high time all honest people were in their beds."—"The devil take you all," vociferated the landlord—"are ye a set of infernals or not?—avaunt!—out of my doors instantly, I say— I'll touch none of your money—away! away!"—So saying, he turned them all out of the door, and locked it after them;—leaving Foote and his companions to proceed peaceably on their journey—the whole having been a laughable contrivance of this modern Aristophanes to get a good supper on the road without paying a farthing for it. (*The Virginia Almanac, for...1799* (34943))

A Gentleman once bought a horse of a country dealer. "Now my friend," (said he) "I have bought your horse because I like his appearance. I asked you no questions.—Tell me now his faults. You know I have paid you; therefore you have nothing to fear." "Faults!" (replied the man)—"I know of no faults, except two." "What are they?"—"Why Sir,—he is bad to catch." "I don't mind that" (said he) "if he be the devil. But what is the other fault?" (rejoined he with some impatience.)—"Ah, Sir," (replied Hodge, scratching his pate)—"He is good for nothing when you have catch'd him!" (*Weatherwise's Massachusetts, Connecticut, Rhodeisland, Newhampshire and Vermont Almanack, for...1799* (34969))

A Gentleman on his travels, called his servant to the side of the post chaise.—"Tom," says he, "here is a guinea which is too light, and I can get nobody to take it, do you see and part with it some how or other on the road"—"Yes, sir," says the footman, "I will endeavor." When they came to their inn at night, the gentleman called the servant to know if he had passed off the guinea? "Yes sir," says the man, "I did it slily." "Aye Tom," says the master, "I fancy thou are a sly sort of fellow; but tell me how?" "Why, sir," says the footman, "the people refused it at breakfast, and so they did where your honor dined; but as I had a groat to pay at the turnpike, I whipped it in between the half pence, and the man put it in his pocket and never saw it." (*An Astronomical Diary, or Almanac, for...1801* (38487))

4. Servants

A peasant carrying, in his master's name, a basket of pears to a nobleman, found two large monkies upon the stairs, with blue cloaths embroidered in gold with swords by their side; they cast themselves upon the basket of fruit. The peasant, who had never seen such animals, took off his hat in a genteel manner to them, and let them do what they pleased. When he had delivered his present the master of the house asked him, "Why did you not bring in a basket quite full?"

"Sir," said the peasant, "it was quite full, but the young gentlemen your children took away the other half from me." (*Father Abraham's Almanack for...'1779*(16050))

After some thieves had robbed a gentleman of a great deal of money, a watch and a ring, and good cloaths, that were in his portmanteau; "Sir," says his man, "must I give them the hundred pounds in gold, too, which is quilted in my breeches?" (*Bickerstaff's Genuine Almanack for.. 1795* (21593))

A gentleman who was passing through the room where his servant was at breakfast, and saw him cut a huge slice off the loaf, asked him, if that bread was not hot?—"No, sir," said the man—"*I thought it was,*" replied his master, "*for you make it smoke, I see.*" (*Banneker's Wilmington Almanac, for...1795* (26613))

An old gentleman having occasion for a footman, desired his nephew to look out for one; and as he could not find any other whom he thought would suit him, he desired his own to hire himself to his uncle. The man, who revered his young master, reluctantly quitted him; but being persuaded it would be for his advantage, he repaired to the old gentleman, who being confident that his nephew would not recommend him an improper person, only asked him, if he understood *sequences*. "I do not know, sir," replied the man; "but if you will be pleased to explain yourself, I hope to be able to give you satisfaction."—"I mean," said the old gentleman, "that when I order you to lay the cloth, you should understand by it all the things connected with it, as the knives, forks, salt, spoons, &c. And so upon all occasions, not to do barely what you are bid, by word of mouth, but to think of the *consequences, sequences,* or dependencies of one thing upon another."

The man assured him that he had not the least doubt of pleasing him: accordingly he was hired, and for some time they agreed perfectly well; but at last his master finding himself suddenly ill, one morning ordered him to fetch a nurse as soon as possible. Instead of returning with speed, he was absent for several hours; and the moment he came into his master's presence, he severely reprimanded him for having staid so long away, when he had sent him on business that required dispatch. The arch fellow waited till the old gentleman's passion was abated, and then proceeded to justify his conduct in the following manner: That he went and found the nurse, who was below: thinking the *consequence* of a nurse might be an apothecary, he had been for one, who was also below; that knowing a doctor always followed an apothecary, he had likewise fetched a physician. A surgeon was often, he said, the *sequence* of a doctor, and an undertaker the *consequence* of all: he had therefore brought them, and hoped he had thoroughly understood his orders."

The old man was so pleased with the humour of the man, that he ordered him to fetch a lawyer to make codicil to his will, by which he left him a valuable legacy. (*Poulson's Town and Country Almanac, for...1798* (32384))

The late benevolent Mr. H. having hired a new coachman, was informing him of the several duties of his office, besides which, he told him that he must attend family prayers every Sunday evening.—"Prayers, Sir," (said John) "what are prayers?"—"Why, did you never say your prayers?" asked Mr. H.—"No," (answer'd the coachman) "I never hired in a praying family."—"Well, but you can have no objection to attend prayers in mine?"—"No," (said Mr. Whip) "if your Honor will consider them in my wages!" (*The Virginia and North Carolina Almanac, for...1800* (35239))

A certain lady of quality spoke to her butler to be very saving of a barrel of good small beer, and asked him how it could be best preserved—the butler replied, " *by placing a barrel of good ale by it.*" (*The Town and Country Almanac, for...1799* (34545))

A Gentleman having put out a candle by accident one night, ordered his waiting man (who was a simple being) to light it again in the kitchen; "but take care, James," added he, "that you do not hit yourself against any thing in the dark."—Mindful of the caution, James stretched out both arms at full length before him, but unluckily, a door that stood half open, passed between his hands and struck him a woeful blow upon the nose; "Dickens!" muttered he, when he recovered his sense a little, "I always heard that I had a plaguy long nose, but I vow I never have thought that it was longer than my arm." (*The Columbian Almanac: or, the North-American Calendar, for... 1799* (33539))

A gentleman being on horseback, his servant, who was on foot, in stroking his horse's buttocks, received a kick: He then aimed a stone at the horse, and hit his master on the back, which made him turn about and ask his man what was the matter. " *Your horse, sir,*" says he, holding out one of his legs, "has lamed me." "Ay," says his master," *he is very unruly, for he has kicked me on the back, 'tis well he missed my head!*" (*Franklin's Legacy: or, The New-York and Vermont Almanack, for... 1799* (34376))

A gentleman and his man riding into the country, they met a fellow astride a cow. The man calls out to his master, "O, Sir," says he, "yonder is a strange sight! a fellow is on horseback on a cow." "That is a bull," said the gentleman. "Nay, Sir," said the man, "it is not a bull, I know it's a cow by its teats." (*The New-England Almanac...for... 1800* (35368))

The errors of simplicity can never excite anger, they may sometimes produce much innocent merriment. A family lately advertised for a wet nurse—a sixteen year old appears; the lady was astonished that she should be qualified to be a wet nurse—"Madam, I never was a wet nurse, but could soon learn to be one." (*An Astronomical Diary, Calendar, or Almanack, for... 1800* (36383))

A dog lying under a table, the maid went to kick him out, and he did not stir: "if a body would kill this dog," says she, "I believe he would not stir from his place." (*The United States Almanac, for... 1801* (36934))

5. Wit

A coxcomb asked a stuttering barber's boy, "did you ever shave a monkey?" "No, sir," said the boy, "but if you will s-s-s-sit down, I'll t-t-try." (*An Astronomical Diary...for... 1793* (24824))

A rich farmer's son who had been at the University, coming home to visit with his father and mother, and being one night at supper with them on a couple of fowls, he told them, that by logic and arithmetic, he could prove these two fowls to be three. "Well, let us hear," said the old man. "Why, this," cried the scholar, "is one, and this," continued he, "is two; two and one, you know make three." "Since you have made it out so well," answered the old man, "your mother shall have the first fowl, I will have the second, and third you may take for your great learning." (*Hutchins Improved: being an Almanack...for...1794* (25646))

As a gentleman in a certain coffee house, was writing a letter to his friend, there being a good deal of company present, a pert young fellow posted himself behind him. The gentleman concluded his letter with these words: " *should write more, but there is an impudent puppy looking over my shoulder.*" The macaroni instantly turned upon his heels, and exclaimed aloud, " *I'll be d--d if I was looking over your shoulder.*" (*Weatherwise's Massachusetts, Connecticut, Rhodeisland, Newhampshire and Vermont Almanack, for...1799* (34969))

A flourishing coxcomb came into a shoemaker's shop to try on a pair of boots. "These are too short for the top," said he, "they should be long enough to cover up the calf completely." "Then," said the shoemaker, "they must be about five feet ten inches." (*The Town and Country Almanac, for...1799* (34545))

6. American pride

Epigram on the British Lion

Our lion once did roar and look so grim,
His very shadow durst not follow him;
But now he is so frighted and dismay'd
He dares not face the shadow of a shade.
(*The Farmer's Diary for...1792* (23496))

Soon after the commencement of the peace, between Britain and America, the master of an American vessel in London, fell in company with some sharpers, who urged him very much to join them in drinking a bottle or two of porter. He, not aware of their policy, consented to go to a public house; where, after they had all drank very freely, they drop't off, one by one, till at last the Yankee was quite alone. The innkeeper coming in says to him, "What! are you left alone?"—"Yes," replied the other. The innkeeper observed to him that he supposed he was not much acquainted with "our English blades."—"I am not," replied the American. "Well," said the innkeeper, "the reckoning falls on you."—"Does it!" replied the other, and clapping his hand to his pocket as if to pay it—but pausing, he says, "Well, if this be the case, give me another bottle before I go." The innkeeper stepped out to get it. In the mean time the American wrote upon the table—"I leave you AMERICAN HANDLES for your ENGLISH BLADES"—and walked off in his turn. (*Carleton's Almanack...for...1794* (25261))

Some officers of the British army who had served during the American war, walking in Hyde-Park dressed in their regimentals, met an American deformed by a haunch on his back when one of them jocularly clapping his hand thereon exclaimed, "What have you got there, my friend?" To which the other with a countenance expressive of the insult, replied, "BUNKER HILL." (*Wait's York, Cumberland and Lincoln Almanack, for...1794* (25733))

Sometime after the conclusion of the late war, a young American was present in a British play-house, where an interlude was performed in ridicule of his countrymen. A number of American officers being introduced in tattered uniforms, and barefoot, the question was put to them severally: "What was your *trade* before you entered into the army?"—One answered, "a *taylor*," another, "a *cobler*," &c.—The wit of the piece was to banter them for not keeping themselves clothed and shod; but before this could be expressed, the American exclaimed from the gallery—"Great Britain beaten by taylors and coblers!—Huzza!"—Even the prime minister, who was present, could not help smiling amidst a general peal of laughter. (*Stoddard's Diary: or, The Columbian Almanack, for...1797* (30048))

Good Advice to Country Politicians

With politics ne'er break your sleep
    But ring your hogs, and shear your sheep,
        And rear your lambs and calves;
And Washington will take due care
    That Briton never more shall dare
        Attempt to make you slaves.
(*The Town and Country Almanack, for...1797* (31616))

The first American vessel that anchored in the river Thames, after the peace, attracted great numbers to see the stripes. A British soldier bullied in a contemptuous tone, "From whence come you, brother jonathan?" The boatswain started, "straight from Bunker's hill, d--n you." (*Beers's Almanac for...1799* (33388))

A Frenchman was travelling in one of the upper countries, not long since. He met one of our young men with his musket and furniture going to attend muster—"Pray, young man," says Monsieur, "be you one *aristocrat* or one *democrat*?" "Why," replied the youth, "I am *superior* to *either,* I am an AMERICAN." (*An Astronomical Diary, or Almanac, for...1799* (34529))

At a review in New-Jersey, during the prevalence of the Yellow Fever at Philadelphia, a number of the Philadelphians were looking at the troops who were paraded--a young Englishman, stepping up to one of the citizens, observed, "they were not English troops." *"No,"* replied the citizen, *"but they* BEAT *them!" (The Starry Calculator; being an Almanac for...1800* (36357)

Chapter Two
The Yankee

The stories of the preceding chapter show how American humor was beginning to group together certain qualities associated with various comic stereotypes. Eventually a new stereotype would emerge. The Yankee, who made a brief appearance in one of the Franklin stories and in the sow in a sack story, was one of the earliest truly American heroes.

Richard Dorson listed nine characteristics that have come to be associated with the Yankee stereotype. The Yankee is not deferential, but is boastful; the Yankee is inquisitive about others, but evasive about himself or herself; he or she is insolent; he or she is a country bumpkin and is naive, is filled with the spirit of American independence, has a heart of gold, moral strength and physical courage.[1]

In the years of the early American republic many American almanacs printed stories about people who were similar to Dorson's characterization of the typical Yankee. Many of the stories, as we have seen, dealt with countrymen or countrywomen. The heroes or heroines were often boastful, naive, inquisitive or evasive. They often demonstrated moral courage and sometimes physical courage. Many of them had a heart of gold.

There was, however, seldom a specifically Yankee type to unify the body of almanac stories. Rather, the almanacs seem to present a body of stories waiting for a hero.

Such a type began to appear in almanac stories during the last years of the century. Perhaps the appearance was most dramatic in the already quoted story of Jonathan and the sow in the sack. The story represents one of the earliest appearances of Jonathan, a name that since Royall Tyler's play The Contrast *had become nearly synonymous with "Yankee." Two years before the version printed in* The Columbian Almanac, *Nathan Daboll's* New England Almanac...for...1799 *(33595) had printed the same story. Daboll's countryman had been named Hodge, and his final speech lacked the American colloquialism of Jonathan's. Popular stories tend to become attached to popular characters or types. By late 1800 "Jonathan" had obviously become a popular enough type to begin to attract a body of stories, one of which appeared in* The Columbian Almanac.

Many of the stories collected in this chapter represent stories that had not yet become attached to Jonathan or the more generic term "Yankee," but with some changes, they finally did. For example, The Spirit of the Times *published "A Melting Story" about a Yankee storekeeper who devised a novel punishment for a person who had stolen some butter from him. It is an excellent story and is well adapted to the Yankee character. It is also a story that was published in a vastly different form more than fifty years earlier in an American almanac. The almanac story is included in this chapter not because it is a Yankee yarn, but because it helped to provide the raw material for the yarn.*

When the good governor Talcott presided over Connecticut, a poor simple man came to him one day, complaining very bitterly of the hardness of the times, and the scarcity of money, and that he was unable to get any, and wondered they did not make money, and would have him use his influence to have a bank made.

After hearing the good man through, he turns to him and asked him if he had any pork or beef to sell? "No." Any wheat or grain of any kind? "No." Any butter, cheese, wool or flax? "for," says the governor, "if you have, I will give you money for them." Why, no, he had not anything to sell. "Then," says the governor, "suppose we should make a bank of paper money, how do you expect to get it?" Why, truly, he did not know. (*The Wilmington Almanack...for...1788* (20366))

The following Advertisement copied from one in the Punch Bowl Tavern in Brookline, we publish for the amusement of our political readers.

To be sold by Lydia Learned,
    in Brookline near the sign of the Punch Bowl,
Flour, raisins, rice, molasses, spice,
    good indigo and wire,
Knives, combs, fish-hooks, ballets and books,
    and paper by the quire,
Sugar biscuit, and chocolate,
    tin, glass, and earthen ware,
Pins, needles, thread, and ginger-bread,
    as good as any where,
Salt, allum, coffee, tea, and snuff,
Crown (soap), and candles, cheap enough,
Buy worth a dollar, when you come,
and you may drink a glass of rum.
(*The Pennsylvania Almanack, for...1788* (20751))

"An Old Woman Basted with Butter"

A poor old woman that lived in the country, just by a nobleman's country seat, was used to go there every day, to do any odd thing about the kitchen, that the cook or his maid, were pleased to set her about, for which they used to send her home with the broken victuals, and which comfortably maintained a brood of grandchildren she had at home, who, otherwise, must have fared but poorly. But, one day, as the old woman was busy poking about the larder, the kitchen maid happening to cast her eye that way, saw her cram a whole lump of butter, consisting of about two pounds weight, into the crown of her high crowned hat, which she (not suspecting that any body saw her) immediately tied upon her head again, with the butter in it; upon which the maid instantly informed the cook of it.—"D--n her dry old head!" (quoth the cook) "it will be cruel to expose the old jade, and deprive her of the benefit of the house, because her poor family at home must suffer for it; but I will punish her severely for it before she goes away"— So the cook and the maid seemed to take no more notice about it; but by-and-by the old woman comes into the kitchen, as she used to do, when she had done all they had set her about, and demanded of the cook, (as per custom)—"Well, my good master, have you any thing more for me to do?"—"No, mother," (replies the cook) "not at present, and here is the broken victuals for you, but be sure that you are here by nine o'clock tomorrow morning."—"Yes, yes," (returns the old woman) "God bless you, my good master! I'll not fail to be sure"—But just as the old woman was got out at the door, and thought herself secure, the cook called her back again. "Mother," (says he) "I lik'd to have forgot, but I must beg one favour of you before you go, yet."—"Ay, ay," (replies the old woman) "what is it, Sir?"—"Why," (says the cook) "only to baste this uppermost spit for me a little, and when you have done, I will give you a dram."—"Thank you kindly, sir!" (says the old woman) "God in Heaven bless you! You are very good."—So down he sets her, before a great kitchen fire, with near two bushels of coals on it, and three or four spits a going, and with the basting ladle cramm'd as full of butter as he could well stuff it. "Here, mother (says the cook) you need only to baste this uppermost spit, and I'll tell you when it is enough."—So the old woman went to work as she was directed, but she had not sat there long, before the butter began to melt in her hat and ran a full stream down her face and neck, into her back and bosom. She wiped her face over and over again, till her handkerchief was as greasy as her head, and then she was forced to take the tail of her gown for the same purpose for her apron was filled with offal and all would not wipe off the butter so fast as it came down her face. The cook (who stood by all the while to observe the operation) was pleased to the heart, to see it work so well; and so salutes her thus: "Well, mother," (says he) "why you sweat, methinks; who would imagine that a woman of your age should have so much grease in her?"—"That's very true," (quoth the old woman) "but to be sure, this fire is very hot; is it not almost basted enough, do you think, Sir?"—"No, no," (replies the cook) "not half enough neither; but come, mother, I'll keep you company a little; don't you be faint-hearted because you sweat a little more than ordinary; it will do you good. Here, Betty," (continued he) "bring the poor old woman a bumper of brandy, that she may warm the inside of her as well as the outside,"—So down he sits himself by her, lest she should take it in her head to pull her hat off before her punishment was compleat. And when he thought that nearly all the butter in her hat was melted away, he released her; but the poor old woman, by this time, was basted all over from head to foot; so he gave her another glass of brandy, and then discharged her; but it happening to be a very keen freezing air, She was no sooner out of the house than she was, as it were, in a moment transported out of the torrid zone into the frigid zone, and covered all over, in ten minutes, with hard butter from head to foot, which made her out a most ridiculous and grotesque figure; and which, without injury to her poor innocent family, might very possibly conduce more to cure her of the vile itch of thieving than a much heavier punishment. (*An Astronomical Diary, Kalendar, or Almanack, for...1788* (20874))

A traveller stopped at a certain inn to dine. When the bill was brought in, (which by the way was lengthy) Mr. Host was asked his name. *"Patridge,* Sir," replied the landlord, "Indeed it ought to have been *Woodcock,* by the length of your bill." (*Father Tammany's Alamanac for...1793* (25059))

A countryman in Birmingham-market, England, was observed to laugh while the clerk was taking a quantity of butter from a woman which was deficient in weight; the officer not being pleased with the fellow's want of decency, observed, "that it ill became him to laugh," adding, "I took two pounds from you last week." "I'll bet a guinea of it," said the countryman. "Done," said the officer, putting a guinea into the hands of an eminent tradesman, the countryman instantly covered it; and then with a sneer said, "Had it been *two pounds* could you have taken it from me? Was it not for being *short* of that weight that I lost it?"—The officer attempted to explain, but the gentleman who held the stakes was so perfectly convinced, that he gave the countryman the stakes immediately. (*The Wilmington Alamanac...for...1794* (25494))

A man who had more pride than taste, calling one cold morning at a tavern for some spirits was told by the landlord he had only New-England rum in his house; at which our traveller was much mortified, observing, he wondered any person could drink such stinking stuff. The woman of the house willing to have some diversion at his expence, observed to him, she had some liquor in a bottle which her husband knew nothing of— "You are the woman for me," says he, "lets have some of it." She brought the bottle which contained no other than New-England Rum, gave him a glass, which he drank, smacking his lips, and praising her West-India rum (as he thought it) paid a West-India price, and went off well satisfied. (*Weatherwise's Almanack for...1795* (28037))

A pious gentleman one Sunday, said,"I vow I won't cut wood today if I cut it in the cellar." (*Stoddard's Diary: or, the Columbia Almanack, for...1796* (29124))

Said a Dutchman to a Yankee, as they were walking on the banks of the Hudson, "How de Devil did dat man, we read of in de Bible, make iron swim?" "It was through Faith," (answered his Comrade); "and" (rejoined he) "if you can but have Faith too, you may make your axe swim." After repeated assurances, the Dutchman said, "Vel I do have Fait vonce;" and, deliberately tossing it into the river saw it go to the bottom: When, turning to his laughing comrade he hastily exclaimed, "Dare now, I *knew* it would sink." "That's the very reason" (said the Yankee): "You did not believe."
"Now I see it, so plain as day," (said the Dutchman): " *But it vas von right Yankee trick.*" (*Dickson's Balloon Almanac, for...1799* (33636))
(The same story also appeared in *Stoddard's Diary* (33391) for the same year where it used the phrase "d—d Yankee trick.")

In the Western territory there lived a man, who went by the name of lazy Charles, who from his youth had required a habit of idleness, and by his much sitting &c. his legs swelled and in consequence of that he employed a physician to cure him of his malady, who told him that he must have some of his water and examine it, accordingly Charles sent some of his water by his girl when she went to drive the cow, who unfortunately spilt it, but soon replaced it by the help of the cow, and on she goes, the Doctor took it, examined it and told the little girl that he would give her daddy an answer in a day or two; he did so as follows, "neighbour Charles thou art with calf, and the 28th of February next, you will produce from your belly a black bull calf." When Charles heard what ailed him, it set him into a convulsion of laughter and broke his spleen intirely, and he became a wholesome inhabitant. And as it happened on that day of February, forgetful of all the the Doctor had told him, he set out to search some deer, it being very cold, and in his travel he came across a man that froze to death, and Charles stript him of everything but his boots, and them he could not get off, so he cut off his legs, and on he goes and being benighted, he got lost, and after wandering a long time, he came at last to a small house, and wished to sleep there, the man told him that he might sleep by the fire, which suited Charles, for he wished to thaw his dead legs, which be brought in and set in the corner. After the people were in bed, the man of the house heard a bellowing in his yard, he gets up to see what the matter was, and behold there was a calf, it being so cold he brought the calf in and put it before the fire on some straw unknown to Charles; in the night Charles awaked and see the calf which brought every thing fresh to his mind that the Doctor had told him and being so frightened to think it had come to pass, that he run and left everything. In the morning the man got up and see the calf tumbling about and nothing to be seen of the man, but his gun, dead legs and hat, he cried out, " *Wife, Wife, we have got the d—l here instead of a calf, and he has eat up the man all but his legs, and them he cannot eat for his boots,*" and catched the gun and shot the calf, bang, "there d—n you, next time eat legs and all." (*Stoddard's Diary; or, the Columbia Almanack, for . . . 1799* (33391))

A Nobleman wishing to have a drawing of his game-keeper with a dog and gun in the act of shooting, sent for a painter, who drew a dog and a great tree. The peer asked him what he had done with his gamekeepr? "He is behind the tree, my lord," answered the painter. "Very true," said his lordship, "he used to stand behind the tree—It is an excellent likeness!" (*An Astronomical Diary, or Almanac, for . . . 1799* (34529))

A fiery English gentleman having challenged a foreign Count, the lodgings of the latter was the place agreed upon for the rencontre. Accordingly, when the Englishman repaired to the rendezvous, he found the Count waiting for him in a small room, of which the whole furniture was a barrel of gunpowder with one head out, two chairs, and a table on which were a lighted candle and a brass farthing, and was instantly addressed as follows: "Come, Sir, toss up that farthing, and see whose lot it shall be to thrust the candle into the powder and blow ourselves into atoms." This address quite staggering the nettlesome blade, the Count seized the candle and brandished it several times over the barrel, frightened him so that he ran off without thinking of demanding any further satisfaction. It is a question of whether this method of terminating duels would not tend to make them somewhat unfashionable. (*Beers's Almanac for . . . 1800* (35164))

Not long since a gentleman from Connecticut, (whom I shall designate by the letter B.)—being on his way to the westward, was stopped in York state, on Sunday, by a miserly Dutchman, who was invested with civil authority. Mr. B. in vain plead the necessity of pursuing his journey unmolested. At length, taking a five dollar bill from his pocket book:— "Sir," said he, "this is at your service, on condition you will give me a *pass."* After a few minutes pause, this mercenary character replied, " *Yes, I will give you von pass for five Tollars*; you may write de pass, and I will make my mark X." Mr. B. accordingly sat down, and drew an order on a merchant in town for 50 dollars in cash and 50 dollars worth of English goods; with the Dutch signature; and takes his leave, with, "Your humble servant"—Calls on the merchant, who cheerfully loaned 50 dollars with the idea of 50 per cent gain on the goods. Soon after, the merchant calls on our noble Dutchman for the balance of the order; at which he started and exclaimed! " *By Cot I oze you noting*, ize give no order on you. If *ize vant any ting* in your store, you know ize got moneys, and *alvays pay."* The merchant produced the order; and on seeing his mark exclaimed! "Dis is dat dam Yankee pass!" But found himself reluctantly obliged to cancel the demand; Swaring *dat if he could see dat dam rascal, he would give him von horse lickin.* (*The New-England Alamanac...for...1800* (35368))

A Gentleman from the southard, some time since, travelling thro New England stopped a number of days at an inn in Connecticut, where, for several nights, he experienced the most assiduous attention from a host of hungry bed-bugs. After a number of attempts to get rid of these friendly visitants, it was discovered that their retreats were in the cracks and crevices of the ceiling. The gentleman, after having his bedstead well cleaned and fresh bedclothes prepared, fell upon the following expedient as the last effort to secure his nocturnal peace:

On going to bed he called for a jug of molasses, and drawing his bedstead into the middle of the chamber, he, with his jug, made, on the floor, a complete ring of molasses round his bed. After laying himself down a few minutes, and anticipating the sweets of undisturbed repose in his fancied security, he observed the bugs mustering from their several retreats and making towards the object of their affection. On arriving at the ring, they immediately stopped and then proceeded to reconoitre, when, finding themselves cut off by this impassable barrier, they retraced their steps to the ceiling, ascended its sides, and marching to the centre of the wall, directly over the bed, whence they deliberately dropped down, one by one, upon the poor out-witted traveller, and soon convinced him, that in *Yankee tricks* he was still inferior to a *New England Bed-bug.* (*The New Jersey and Pennsylvania Almanac, for...1800* (36305))

A woman, a few months ago, went into a tavern, called for a gill of New England rum and drank it. Upon which the lady, who tended the bar, expressed her wonder that she should drink so much rum on an empty stomach—"Why la!" says she, "my stomach is not empty, *for I drank a pint before this very morning!"* (*The Starry Calculator; being an Almanac for...1800* (36357))

Chapter Three
The Tall Tale

A paragraph in the Citizen and Farmers Almanac, *for 1801 showed a real understanding of a tall tale. The paragraph reported a high wind that had blown seven calves out of the cow house and over a hedge without doing them any harm and which had also blown a duck's head off. The paragraph concludes "To have made the account quite complete, the wind should have blown the calves back again into the cow-house, and the duck's head on again."*

If the story of the remarkable wind had ended as the writer suggested, it would have fit the mold of one type of tall tale, the type that, perhaps, is most recognizable today. It begins with realistic details and gradually stretches the belief of the listener and reader. Finally, it completely breaks the boundaries of belief with a capper. The story of a man caught between a bear and an alligator is a good example. When told, the story often begins with an account of the man's meeting with a bear, a realistic possibility. The man flees. This is to be expected. He comes to a river containing a huge alligator, a somewhat improbable coincidence. He is afraid to jump into the river, so he falls to the ground. The bear leaps for him, misses, and tumbles into the river. Credulity is now stretched to its limit. The bear and the alligator devour each other. At last we have reached the "capper" of the piece. The utterly impossible conclusion lets the audience know the whole story was a lie all along.

If this is the pattern of the tall tale, then American almanacs of the early republic contain few tall tales. They do, however, contain the material out of which tall tales could be made, as the writer of the Citizen and Farmer's *paragraph recognized. There is, for example, a story of a man pursued by a tiger in India. He ducks as the tiger leaps and the tiger falls into a river where it battles a crocodile as the man makes his escape. The teller of the tiger-crocodile story obviously hoped to be believed. The teller of the bear-alligator story expected that he would be believed for a while, but that finally the audience would recognize the hoax.*

TALL TALES

A. Beasts and Monsters

The Majestic Mermaid
A Sea Monster
Lately seen on the Coast of BARBARY, by the people on board the
AMERICAN Brigantine, COLUMBIA, Captain HARDY.

On the 4th of July, at nine o'clock A.M. being in lat. 25, lon. 33,
sailing with a pleasant breeze and a smooth sea, we suddenly descried a
surprising agitation of the water, a small distance ahead, which in a moment,
spread a violent convulsion over a large expanse of the sea, and gave a
shock to our vessel much like that of an earthquake. Our helm was no
longer of service, so great was the agitation of the water, when to add to
our consternation, a terrific monster, of gigantic size, and various appearances
raised its awful form to an amazing height above the surface of the ocean,
and passing with incredible celerity round our vessel, seem'd to view us
with great attention.

The stoutest heart on board was for a while sunk with apprehension
of immediate dissolution, but finding no violence offered to the vessel, by
the monster, reflection soon got the better of their fears, and enabled them
to pay a degree of attention to the form of the being which had occasioned
such universal dismay.

He was part man and part woman, blended variously as to the
body and face, his size enormous, and from the naval to the top of his
head appear'd about forty feet, the lower part of his body was covered with
scales like a fish, and appeared, through the transparency of the water, of
much greater length than was visible above the surface, terminating in a
tail which he occasionally used to keep himself floating. His head was formed
with four different faces, bespeaking rage, tranquility, deformity and beauty.
On the top of his head was a large eye, encircled by a rising cressence
something like a crown, in the centre of each face was a brilliant eye, which
conjunctively with that on the head, when he arose from, sank to, or reclined
on the surface of the water, made a very splendid appearance like that of
the sun when setting. Beneath each eye was a regular nose, mouth and chin,
each muscle conformable to its particular face. The faces were of different
complexions, *viz.* fair, swarthy, tawny and black, his neck, one shoulder,
one breast, arm and hand was like those of a woman, the other like those
of a man; from his wrists to his body, under his arms were [   ] membranous
wing, like the fin of a fish. From the protruberance of his hips there were
two large fins, which he kept in motion to bouy himself up. The brilliancy
of his scales formed a most beautiful variegation of colours in the water,
some being in appearance like, though more magnificent than, the rainbow.

We were filled with admiration at the tremendous size and majestic appearance of this surprizing phaenomenon, when on a sudden we were almost petrified with fear, by a voice like thunder; issuing from the mouth of Deformity, articulating in tremendous accents, "WOE, WOE, WOE, to the INHABITANTS of the WORLD, for the Demon of DISCORD is busy upon the EARTH, EUROPE is verging to BLOODY WARS, to despotism and decay. ASIA and AFRICA are sinking under the accumulated burthens of EUROPEAN TYRANNY, native IGNORANCE, and the most absurd IDOLATRY." "and AMERICA," said the angry countenance, "so lately and so highly favoured is even now in a state of anarchy and division."

"You are highly favored, Oh! AMERICANS," said the tranquil face, "with SAGES whose wisdom has astonished the World, with GENERALS whose prowess shall stand without compare on the records of FAME; with ARTISTS whose ingenuity cannot be exceeded; with PHILOSOPHERS, POETS, and HISTORIANS whose profound wisdom, sublime imagination and deep erudition do honor to their country; with a soil, luxurious, almost beyond compare, and with a RELIGION that will stand the test of AGES."

"Under all these advantages," said the beautiful face, "You need only RESOLUTION to be a PECULIARLY HAPPY PEOPLE. Exert yourselves in promoting the USEFUL ARTS, MANUFACTURES and AGRICULTURE, be UNITED, repose confidence in your RULERS, and keep at all times an EYE towards HEAVEN. Then shall all nations, kindred and complexions yield to America the palm of PRAISE, and animated by so sublime an example, shall study the arts of PEACE and HARMONY and LEARN WAR NO MORE."

"Then the foretold Milenium shall commence,
And joys sublime succeed the joys of sense."

The monster at these words sank from our view, and we pursued our course without further interruption. (*The Universal Calendar, and the North-American Almanack, for...1788* (20726))

In February, 1794, near Kentucky, a detachment of mounted infantry commanded by Capt. John Beiard, penetrated fifteen miles into the Cumberland Mountains on Cove Creek. Ensign M'Donald and another man, in advance of the party as spies, discovered a creature about three steps from them; it had only two legs, and stood almost upright, covered with scales of a black, brown, and a light yellow colour, in spots like rings, a white tuft or crown on the top of its head, about four feet high, a head as big as a two pound stone, and large eyes of a fiery red. It stood about three minutes in a daring posture, orders being given out not to fire a gun except at Indians, Mr. M'Donald advanced and struck it with his sword, when it jumped up at least eight feet, and lighted on the same spot of ground, sending forth a kind of matter out of its mouth resembling blood, and then retreated into a laurel thicket, turning round often, as if it intended to fight. The tracks of it resembled that of a goose, but larger. The Indians report that a creature inhabits that part of the mountain of the above description, which by its breath will kill a man, if he does not instantly immerse himself in water. (*Greenleaf's New-York, Connecticut and New-Jersey Almanack for...1795* (26634))

B. Remarkable Behavior by Animals

There is an account of an Adventure (than which one will scarce find any Thing more surprizing) in a journal belonging to the Dutch East-India Company certified by the whole Ship's Crew before the Judges of the Admiralty at Amsterdam. This Ship having Cast Anchor in the River Ganges, sent out a Boat, with eight Mariners, to catch Fish; as they were casting their Nets, one of the Men got out of the Boat, and climbed up the Bank, either led by a Desire to view the Country, or some other Design; but he had not gone on it above twenty paces, when he perceived a Crocodile very near him: Terrified at this bitter enemy of mankind, whom he saw getting up the Bank towards him, he thought to save himself by getting down on the other Side; but at that very Instant he saw a Tyger rush out of an adjacent Forest, and run with his usual swiftness towards him. Either his Fear or his Prudence put it into his Head to throw himself flat on the Ground, and the Tyger, having taken his Race with too precipitous a Force, flew directly over him, and fell into the River, where the Crocodile, flying on this new Adversary, dragged him with him into the Middle of the Stream: The Mariner, delivered by so Strange a Change rejoined his Comrades, who with Fear and Wonder had beheld all that had passed. (*Hutchins Improved...for...1780* (16308))

A Gentlemen on the road to the house of a friend, was on a sudden seized by such an unexpected eruption of disorderly matter from the prison of his tormented bowels as an explosion from the mouth of Aetna, did the fatal business before he had warning to provide for his deliverance. His storm blasted gal gaskins were outrageously torn off, and were most inhumanly buried in the sepulchre of the next ditch, which were succeeded in the throne by a fresh pair from his portmanteau. All was appeased and easy: But mark the catastrophe! Scarce was he sat down to the refreshments of a friendly dinner and engaging company, but the suffusion of a Tartarian vapor spread discord and insurrection all round the table, when the unfortunate gentlemen casting his bewildered eyes to the earth, with the horrors of a guilty Macbeth, discovered just under his chair an apparition of his evil genius, the ghastly spectre of his murdered breeches which a careful spaniel, his attendant, in concern for the extravagance of his prodigal master, had thought a part of the baggage, and delivered to his custody. The sympathizing guests, in tears of laughter, pitied the confusion of the dismayed adventurer, and did not forget to reward honest Ranger's diligence with the remains of the feast, for his exemplary fidelity. (*Bickerstaff's New England Almanac, for...1782* (17429))

  Captain A.P. of Connecticut, several years since having in the same vessel made a number of voyages to the West Indies, and being greatly troubled with the vast number of rats, which he had on board, resolved on adopting some method to get rid of those troublesome adventurers. The mate was ordered to draw the vessel off a little distance from the wharf, extending a plank from the extreme end of the wharf on to the gunnel of the vessel, then with some combustables to make as large a smoke as possible in the hold of the vessel. This method of proceeding produced the desired effect— the rats in great numbers, leaving the hold of the vessel, went off by the plank to a store on the wharf. Among the number that left that vessel, there was one, who, from his appearance had arrived at a very great age, he being blind, as the by-standers judged, with both eyes, his hair on almost every part of him having turned white—this venerable rat held across his mouth a stick about six inches in length; two other rats, one on each side of him, having hold of each end of the stick, led him out with the most attentive circumspection, very slowly, from the vessel on to the wharf, and from thence under the store. The people present (there being a number of gentlemen who saw it) were struck with amazement at beholding this singular respect, shewn by these brutish animals to their aged decrepid ancestor, which was not exceeded even by the famed Eneas of old.(*Carleton's Almanack- ...for...1793* (24177))

  If contemplation is the effect of sense, and sense arises from a soul, we may candidly allow *that* attribute to the brute.—The following extraordinary fact may illustrate the hypothesis, which we had from a gentleman in the state of Maryland, who is curious in raising fowls. One of his hens, though in the midst of summer, had for several weeks stopped yielding her usual produce, and yet daily made her natural cackling. He searched her nest, but could not even find a shell of an egg, which made him resolve to watch her closely. He, accordingly, the next day, situated himself in such a manner as to observe her motions minutely; when, to his great surprise, he saw her laying an egg; but no sooner was she off her nest than three rats made their appearance. One of them immediately laid himself on his back, whilst the others rolled the egg upon his belly which he clasped between his legs, and held very firm; the other two then laid hold of his tail, and gently dragged him out of sight. This wonderful sagacity was exhibited for several days to some curious observers. (*Carleton's Almanack...for...1793* (24177))

A Singular Instance of Sagacity in a Dog
    A gentleman of Suffolk being on a journey, had a dog which he asserted would fetch anything he was ordered from any distance. To prove this, a marked shilling was put under a large square stone on the side of the road, and the gentleman, accompanied by the dog, rode forward for three miles, when the dog's master ordered him to go back and fetch the shilling he had put under the stone. The dog turned back and the gentleman rode forward and got home; but contrary to expectation, the quadruped did not return for the whole day.
    It appeared afterwards that he had gone to the place where the shilling was deposited, but the stone being too large for his strength to remove, he had staid howling at the place until two horsemen riding by, attracted by his seeming distress stopped to look at him, and one of them lighted and moved the stone, when finding the shilling, he put in into his pocket, not conceiving that the dog could be looking for that. The dog followed their horses for upwards of twenty miles, staid in the room where they supped, following the chambermaid into the bed room and hid himself under one of the beds. The possessor of the shilling hung his breeches upon a nail by the bed side, but when they were both asleep, the dog got them off the nail, and the window being open, leaped out with the breeches in his mouth, and dragged them through bog and quagmire, over ditch and hedge, until four o'clock, when he arrived at his master's house. In the pockets were found several guineas and four watches, the owner being a dealer in those articles, and the marked shilling. The watches, &c. being advertised were returned, and the thief was not indicted. (*The Columbian Alamanac...for...1794* (25316))

Remarkable Instance of Sagacity in an Elephant
    Many surprising anecdotes have been related of that half reasoning animal the elephant; but the following is so extraordinary a fact, that had it not occurred in the presence of a numerous body of men, some doubts might arise in the mind of the reader, respecting the credibility of the narration. Among the elephants that went round to Madras with troops in the year 1781, under the command of the late Colonel Pearse, there was one whose keeper had been at times particularly neglectful of him; and who had frequently pilfered from his grain on the line of march. Upon every such occasion the elephant discovered evident signs of anger and resentment, as if he was neither insensible to the negligence nor ignorant of the mal-practices of his keeper. But as the noble minded animal continued but to threaten, the fellow became less and less mindful of him, till at length

he wholly disregarded the frequency of his threats. One morning the cattle, &c. were ordered to be mustered for review, and when the commanding officer, in going along the line, passed in front of the elephant, the animal roared out as if it would seem to attract his attention: for when he perceived that the eye of the colonel was directed towards him, he immediately laid hold of his keeper with his proboscis, put him under his feet, and crushed him to death; then fell upon his knees, and solicited the colonel for pardon. The singularity of this act induced Colonel Pearse to make an immediate enquiry respecting it, when he learnt that the elephant had been forced contrary to his natural disposition, to inflict this punishment on his keeper, for the incorrigible neglect he was prone to commit, and the fraud he had so long practised on his daily allowance. (*Bannaker's Maryland, Pennsylvania, Delaware, Virginia, Kentucky and North Carolina Almanac...for...1796* (28231))

A man on Cape-Cod was hunting near the seashore, a few years since, and discovered a flock of wild geese on the surface of the water. He was waiting for them to advance a little that he might have a better opportunity for shooting. In the meantime, his curiosity was excited by the quick movement of a bunch of seaweed, contrary to that of the tide, and directly towards the geese. He watched its motion till it had gotten to them, without being able to solve the paradox. The geese, to all appearance were not alarmed, until a fox had seized one of them by the neck. The mystery was then unfolded. This subtle quadruped, in order to swim to his booty unobserved, had adopted an expedient so curious and rational as that of wrapping up his visible part in a cloke of sea-weed. Reynard secured the goose, and in a few moments the Huntsman secured him. (*An Astronomical Diary, or Almanack, for...1796* (29493))

A toad was seen to fight with a spider in Rhode Island; and when the former was bit, it hopped to a plantain leaf, bit off a piece, and then engaged with the spider again. After this had been repeated sundry times, a spectator pulled up the plaintain, and put it out of the way. The toad, on being bit again, jumped to where the plantain had stood; and as it was not to be found, she hopped round several times, turned over on her back, swelled up, and died immediately.—This is an evident demonstration that the juice of the plantain is an antidote against the bites of those venomous insects. (*Poor Robin's Almanac, for...1797* (30500))

The Bear

Not long after the settlement of this country, a saw mill was erected in the southern part of Norton. The audacity and singular fate of a bear at the place, on a certain time, merit a place in the cabinet of the virtuoso.

The sawyer had just fixed a log in the carriages, and was sitting on it busily engaged in eating some bread and cheese. A bear at that instant came in without hesitancy, sat down very independently between the man and the saw, and partook with the greatest freedom in the repast. The sawyer could not conveniently encounter him without hazard. Besides, he was well satisfied in his own mind from his knowledge of the innate revengeful disposition incident to this species of animals how his fate would soon turn. The event showed the rationality of his inference. They continued mutually to participate in the portion, till the [log] by its gradual movement had carried the bear to the teeth of the saw. A full stroke on his posteriors brought his ire to the high pitch. He instantly turned about, *grasped the rending saw with all his might, and hugged it till sawn in pieces.* (*An Astronomical Diary or Almanack for...1797* (31613)

As a servant was opening some very large oysters in a gentleman's house in Liverpool, he found one of them with two mice within; one seemed to be dying at the time the oyster was opened, but the other was quite dead. The servant immediately sallied forth to his master, to shew him so strange a sight, who after viewing it a while, supposed that the oyster had opened itself, and the mice, mistaking it for their holes, had crept in, when the oyster feeling such a weight, shut itself so fast as to squeeze and keep them in the manner they were found. (*The Farmer's Calendar; or, Fry and Southwick's Almanack, for...1798* (33172))

A Pleasant Story
    (From Graham's Descriptive Sketch of Vermont)
    The following anecdote of an honest farmer, (one of the first settlers) which happened at *Westminster*, will serve to show the fanatical spirit which then prevailed—so contrary to that liberal toleration now prevalent over America—and which so happily unites every denomination of Christians in the bonds of Charity and love,—but to my story.
    The farmer in question was a plain, pious man, regular in the discharge of his duty both to God and his neighbour; but unluckily he happened to live near *one* with whom he was not inclined to cultivate either civil or friendly terms: this troublesome personage was no other than a monstrous over-grown he-bear, that descended from the mountains, trod down and destroyed the corn-fields, and carried off whatever he laid his paws upon. The plundered sufferer watched him in vain, the ferocious and cunning animal was ever finding methods to elude his utmost vigilance; and at last the bear had learned his cue so thoroughly as to commit his depredations only on the Lord's day, when he knew from experience the coast was clear. Wearied out with these oft-repeated trespasses, the good man resolved on the next Sunday to stay in the fields, where, with his gun,

he would conceal himself. The bear came according to custom—he fired and shot him dead. The explosion threw the whole congregation (for it was about the hour of people's assembling to worship) into consternation. The cause was enquired into: and as soon as the Pastor, Deacon and Elders became acquainted with it, they called a special meeting of the church, and cited their offending brother before them, to show cause, if any he had, why he should not be excommunicated out of Christ's church, for this daring and unequalled impiety. In vain did he urge from the Scriptures themselves, that it was lawful to do good on the sabbath-day; he pleaded before judges determined to condemn him; and the rightgeous Parson, Elers and Church, *una voce*, agreed to drive him out from among them as polluted and accursed. Accordingly he was enjoined (as is customary on such occasions) on the next Sunday to attend his excommunication in the church.

He did attend—but, not entirely satisfied with his sentence, and too much of a soldier to be so scandalized in so public a manner for an action which he believed to be a good one, he resolved to have recourse to a strategem: he therefore went as he was summoned, with his gun, loaded with a brace of balls, his sword and cartridge-box by his side, and his knapsack on his back, with six days provisions in it. Service was about half over when he entered the sanctuary in martial array. He marched leisurely into a corner, and took his Position. As soon as the benediction was ended, the holy parson began his excommunication, but scarce had he uttered the words "Offending brother," when the honest veteran cocked and levelled his weapon of destruction, at the same time crying out with a loud voice, " *Proceed if your dare...proceed...and you are a dead man.*"—At this unexpected attack, the astonished clergyman shrunk behind his desk, and his opponent with great deliberation *recovered* his arms. Some minutes elapsed before the Parson had courage to peep from his ecclesiastical battery, when finding the old hero had come to a *rest*, he tremblingly reached the order to the oldest Deacon, desiring him to read it. The Deacon, with stammering accents, and eyes staring wild affright, began as he was commanded; but no sooner had he done so than the devoted victim again levelled his piece and more vehemently than before exclaimed, " *Desist, and march—I will not live with shame; desist, and march, or you are all dead men.*"

Little need had he to repeat his threats: the man of God leaped from his desk and escaped; the Deacon, Elders and congregation followed in equal trepidation; the greatest confusion prevailed, the women with shrieks and cries sought their homes and the victor was left undisturbed master of the *field* and of the *church* too, the doors of which he calmly locked, put the keys in his pocket, and sent them with his respects to the parson. He then marched home with all the *honours of war*, lived thirteen years afterwards, and died a brother in full communion, declaring to the last, (among his intimates) that he never tasted so great a dainty before. (*Hutchins Improved: Being an Almanack and Ephemeris, for...1801* (37669))

C. Remarkable Behavior by Humans

Old Haywood had two daughters by his first wife, of which the eldest was married to John Cahick, the son, and the youngest was married to John Cahick, the father. This Cahick, the father, had a daughter by his first wife, whom old Haywood married, and by her had a son: therefore, Cahick, the father's second wife could say as follows:

My father is my son, and I my mother's mother;
My sister is my daughter; I'm grandmother to my brother.
(*The Wilmington Almanac...for...1794* (25494))

In Enfield, in the upper part of New-Hampshire as two men were crossing a pond in pursuit of a moose, one of them, being thirsty, and perceiving a hole which had been cut through the ice by some fisherman, he stooped down to drink; but being possessed of a long red nose, the fish supposed he had some bait, and made bold to snap at it; when the man suddenly pulling his head back, drew out a perch which weighed three pounds four ounces.
(*The Wilmington Almanac...for...1794* (25494))

Powers of Imagination

In the year 1775, a farmer of Bucks County, Pennsylvania, assisted by his people, working in harvest, killed a rattle snake; and soon after, having occasion to go home, took up by mistake his son's jacket, and put it on; the son was a stripling, and both their jackets were made of the same kind of cloth. The old man being warm, did not button the jacket till he got to the house, then found it much too little for him; he instantly conceived the idea, that he had been imperceptibly bitten by the rattle-snake, and swelled from the effects of the poison. He grew suddenly very ill, and was put to bed. The people about him were very much alarmed; and sent for two or three physicians; one of whom poured down his throat a pint of melted lard—another gave him a dose of wild plantain—and the third made him drink hoar-hound tea, made very strong. Notwithstanding all, he grew worse, and was to all appearance on the verge of dissolution, when the son came home, with the old gentleman's jacket hanging like a bag about him.— The whole mystery was at once unravelled, and the poor farmer, notwithstanding his drenches of hog's fat, plantain, and hoar-hound, was well in an instant. (*Stoddard's Diary: or, the Columbia Almanack, for...1798* (31788))

A pedantic gentleman who was travelling, and above common language, stopped at an inn to get his horse and himself refreshment. Seeing some boys when he alighted, ordered one to circumambulate his quadruped two or three times about the mansion, then permit him to inhale a moderate quantity of aqueous particles, after which to give him proper vegetable nutriment, and he would make him pecuniary satisfaction. The boy being unaccustomed to such language, run into the house and told his father a prince was without doors, who spoke French: the father comes out and hearing the man scold, asked him what was the matter? "Sir," says the gentleman, "I invoke all genii astestis's, that your offspring rejected me, and refused to put into practice my desires. Now, Sir, you I implore to enforce obedience upon them by correction—and then immediately to provide me some nutrious substance, to strengthen nature, cured over vegetable fuel, as I abhor the sulphurious tincture of minerals—remember to get me some stimulus with it."—The inn-keeper, without much hesitation, concluded him a madman, and with his lusty wife seized and tied him hands and feet, to a ring in the barn floor, then went for a doctor, who put a moderate blister on his back, which in three days brought him his wandering senses. (*Stoddard's Diary: or, the Columbia Almanack, for...1798* (31788))

D. Remarkable Natural Phenomena

A late emigrant from Britain, boasting to an American farmer of the vast superiority of that country over this, in arts, sciences, natural productions, &c. by way of proof asked him (pointing to the moon) "What do you call that?" "I call it the moon," said the farmer—"That a moon," rejoins the Englishman, "I'll be damned if the stars in England are not larger!!!" (*The Starry Calculator; being an Alamanc for...1799* (34596))

An Article in a paper stated that a high wind had blown seven calves out of the cow-house, over a hedge twenty yards, without doing them any harm; and that it had also blown a duck's head off! A correspondent who had seen the article, and deeming it a *Munchausen* says, "To have made the account quite complete, the wind should have blown the calves back again into the cow-house, and the duck's head on again." (*Bonsal and Niles' Citizen and Farmers Almanac, for...1801* (37185))

E. The Supernatural

In the year 1751, when the waters of Glastonbury were supposed to be endowed with a supernatural power, and to have been discovered by a revelation from heaven, made in a dream to one Mathew Chancellor, the common people did [not] only expect to be cured of such distempers as were in their nature incurable, but even to recover their lost eyes and mutilated limbs. The following story, among several others, was related by a gentleman of character: An old woman in the workhouse of Yeouil, who had long been a cripple and made use of crutches, was strongly inclined to drink the Glastonbury waters, which she was sure would cure her of her laments. The master of the workhouse accordingly procured her several bottles of water, which [had] such an affect she soon laid aside one crutch, and, not long after, the other. This was extolled as a miraculous cure. But the man protested to his friends that he had imposed upon her, and she had the water from a common spring! It will, perhaps, be needless to add that, when the sense of imagination had spent its power, she slipped in to her former infirmity. (*Bickerstaff's New-England Almanack for...1776* (14066))

Money Digging

A Mr. Z——, native of Mayne, being far from home, and much fatigued, repaired, towards evening, to a lonely mansion. On his approach he discovered a person, with a dejected countenance, just removing the last of his household furniture. Without enquiring either the cause of his melancholy, or removal, Mr. Z humbly requested that during the approaching night his weary limbs might rest under that roof. The stranger expressed an unwillingness. Our traveller repeated his request—alledging that he was a great distance from home, and knew not where to seek shelter. The person at length consented, and in a pensive tone, informed him why he had at first refused to comply with his desire, *to wit*—That the house was haunted with evil spirits—that frightful figures had been seen, noises heard &c. &c.— adding that if he chose, after this information to tarry there, he should be welcome; and further, that in such a chamber was a bed at his service, which, standing in a part of the house frequented by ghosts and devils, he dared not remove it.

Mr. Z kindly thanked him—said he had done no harm to any of his fellow men, and was therefore under no apprehensions from them: As to the Devil, as he had hitherto had no personal acquaintance with him, a sight of him would be by no means disagreeable. The owner of the house, astonished at his fool-hardiness, left him to the mercy of the infernals. Mr. Z. retired to his chamber—reclined himself on the bed, and slept, undisturbed, 'til towards midnight—When—(tremble reader!) to his unutterable surprise, he heard the door next the high way, which he had with his own hand carefully secured, burst open; a *something*, with hideous groans, and steps of terror, ascended the stairs leading to his apartment—the door of which, receiving but one hollow blow, instantaneously gave way—a tall meagre figure, clad in the garments of death, presented itself. Our traveller, in the name of Him who governs ghosts, devils and men, demanded his business. "It is well that you have spoken," replied the deathly visitor: "the errand that I shall now deliver, I have long sought an opportunity to communicate; but the cowardice or wickedness of those I have hitherto accosted, have prevented—they dared not to speak, but fled; and ghostly diffidence suffered me not to call after them.—To you, therefore, I will disclose the secret, that I may rest in the tomb long since allotted me."—His Ghost-ship proceeded: "While on earth I lived a miser—I treasured up riches, not knowing who should gather them. Ere the cold touch of death reached me, I deposited all in that Earth to which I myself was hastening—Follow me—" Mr. Z obeyed—who presently found himself in the center of a large field—"Here," said the Phantom. Pointing downward, "Under this turf—to you I bequeath it—DIG, or never obtain."—An instant and unoccupied space surround our traveller—the spectre fled—Destitute of *digging utensils*—a stranger to the spot, and even to the field, what was to be done?—Postpone *digging* until morning, and leave a *mark*: But here another difficulty arose. What *mark* could he devise that would infallibly designate this, from all other parts of the large enclosure. Besides, there was neither stick nor stone within his reach—nor dared he to remove his foot from the happifying spot, if he did, all was lost. Despair, for a moment, rested on his countenance. But, an ingenious imagination, *assisted by the pressing calls of nature*, put him in a way— *He built an altar to Cloacine, and sacrificed thereon*; in other words, he *did his need*: After leaving his *mark*, he retired to rest. In the morning, the first idea that presented to his enraptured mind was that of the Treasure. "Now," said he, "I will arise, procure, and secret it—none shall see, or share with me." He said, and was about to leap upon the floor— But, gentle Reader, judge of his surprise—when he found the *sacrifice* he had offered—the fancied *Mark*—the very *Need* itself, smoking at his Breech!! (*Weatherwise's Almanack, for . . . 1787* (20124))

Chapter Four
Ethnic and Racial Humor

The people in America during the early republic were made up of a wide variety of ethnic and racial stocks. James Fenimore Cooper's The Pioneers *is set during these years and attempts to present the wide diversity of Americans. Monsieur LeQuoi is presented as an example of the thousands of Frenchmen who emigrated to America during the French Revolution; Major Hartmann is an example of the American "High Dutchers." Benjamin Penguillan is Cornish. Agamemnon is black. Milligan is Irish, and Chingachgook is an American Indian. Judge Templeton and his family are of British descent.*

The nature of American society and its rich racial and ethnic mix provided a fertile field for the development or importation of racial and ethnic humor or dialect stories. In early America the most common groups to appear in dialect stories in almanacs were the Irish, the American Indians, the blacks, and the Germans or Dutch. A few stories dealt with the French, the Jews, the Welch and various other groups. Many of the stories attempted to create the dialect of the ethnic or racial character presented.

Two kinds of dialect stories are presented. In one, the storyteller uses his or her own voice until it is time to deliver the punch line which is emphasized by placing it in the dialect of the character. The other kind is comparatively rare and might be called a dialect tour-de-force. *In the rarer story, the speaker or writer presents a fairly long story entirely in the dialect of the major character.*

Obviously, the dialect stories all present racial or ethnic stereotypes. Sometimes the stereotypes conflict with one another. Such conflict seems especially obvious in the stories told about the American Indian and the black. In each case, some of the stories are sympathetic toward these members of an exploited race and some are less than sympathetic.

Some major characteristics of the Irish stereotype included stupidity, especially the kind of stupidity that led to statements incorporating a kind of comic absurdity called a "bull" or "Irish bull." The Random House Dictionary *defines "bull" as "exaggerations; lies; nonsense," and speculates that it may be a shortened form of "bullshit." Noah Webster's* American Dictionary of the English Language *gives what appears to be a more accurate contemporary definition of "bull: a blunder or contradiction; more exactly, an apparent congruity, but real incongruity of ideas, suddenly discovered."[1]*

The Irishman was also stereotyped as lacking in regard for the law, as belligerent, as a fortune hunter and as a trickster. His dialect includes characteristic phrases such as "By St. Patrick," "Arrah," "By my jewels" and "at all at all." Some writers used misspellings to indicate their conception of Irish pronunciation. "Peach" is spelled "pache." "Devil" is spelled "divel;" "gentleman," "jontleman" and "impertinent" "impartinent." The characteristic Irish name was "Paddy" or some other form of "Patrick."

The black was not as popular a stereotypical figure in American almanacs as was the Irishman, but there were still many stories concerning blacks. Several of them may have originated in America, but, given the interchangeable nature of dialect stories, many others may simply have transferred a story from some other racial or ethnic group to a black. There are five major types of stories about blacks. One portrays blacks as noble savages, another as fools, another emphasizes their role as American slaves, a fourth portrays them as tricksters and the fifth portrays them as wits. There is overlapping among the types of stories. For example, the trickster uses his ability in order to alleviate some of the hardships of slavery, and the noble savage demonstrates his nobility even though he is in the degraded position of slave.

Many of the black stories are told in dialect, but the black dialect is different from the Irish dialect in that it relies more on misspellings to indicate pronunciation and very little on characteristic phrases. "St" is often spelled "t" or "ss" as in "top" or "Massa." "Th" is often spelled "dd" or "t" as in "tudda." "Ee" is often added to the end of a verb, as in "workee." Dialect writers also attempted to distinguish a grammatical difference between black and white English. In some stories "be" is used where most English speakers would use another form of the verb. Articles are commonly omitted, and the black person is commonly shown as referring to himself in the third person.

Like the Irishman, the black was often given distinctive and identifying names. "Quash," "Quashi," "Caesar," "Cato" and "Pompey" were typical.

Of the several racial and cultural groups treated in American almanacs, perhaps the one group whose image is most variable is the American Indian. The Indians lived in America before white people did. Whites had to take their land either by trickery, by force or by honest agreement. Some of the stories express a feeling of guilt over the way Indians were treated, others seem to attempt to justify the behavior of whites and still others show the Indians fighting back by using trickery or wit of their own. American Indians are seldom portrayed as speaking in dialect, nor are they often named. When they are named, there seems to be no stereotypical characterization.

Other ethnic and national groups appear from time to time in almanacs of the early American republic. They include the Dutch or Germans, the Welch, the French and even the Chinese. Comic misspellings and grammar are sometimes present in these stories. It is difficult to generalize about stereotypes from so few examples, but the Dutch or Germans appear fond of the tavern and the Welch appear both poor and belligerent.

THE IRISH

A. The Irish Bull

One Irishman said to another, on hearing peace proclaimed, "Arrah, now, but the Devil burn me, if ever I think the French will be at PEACE at all at all, 'till there's another WAR." (*Thomas's Massachusetts, Connecticut, Rhode-Island, Newhampshire & Vermont Almanack-...for...1789* (21115))

An ignorant preacher in Ireland observed to his hearers that religion had arisen to such a low ebb, and that prophanity was so prevalent than even little children, before they could walk or speak, were running about the streets blaspheming their Maker! (*The Lady's Astronomical Diary, or Almanack, for...1792* (23485))

One Irishman meeting with another, asked him, what was become of their old acquaintance Patrick Murphy? "Arrah! now dear honey," (answered the other) "he was condemned to be hanged, but saved his life by dying in prison." (*An Almanack...for...1792* (25381))

Captain Christie, an Irish officer, who served with considerable credit in America, had the misfortune to be dreadfully wounded in one of the battles there. As he lay on the ground, an unfortunate soldier who was near him, and also much wounded, made a terrible howling, when he exclaimed, "D—n your eyes, what do you make such a noise for, do you think nobody is killed but yourself." (*The Kentucky Almanac, for...1794* (25688))

A gentleman having a Hibernian servant, sent him to drown a dog that was troublesome; on the servant's return, the master asked him whether he had drowned the dog? "Yes, sir," says Patrick, "he is *drowned*, for I stoned him to death." (*The Columbian Almanac: or, the North-American Calendar, for...1795* (26786))

An Irish schoolmaster, from a conviction of the efficacy of *Sunday* schools wants to teach one twice a week—every *Wednesday* and *Saturday*. (*The Columbian Almanac... for...1796*(28450))

On the banks of a rivulet in the north of Ireland is a stone with the following inscription..."Take notice, that when this stone is out of sight, it is not safe to ford the river." (*Poor Richard Revived: being the Farmer's Diary...for...1797* (31099))

An Irishman in North Carolina, had a negro slave who was rather neglectful of business, and would sometimes absent himself from the service of his master, who one morning ordered him upon some business in haste; but seeing him rather slow, Paddy came to him in a violent passion, and said, "You black rascal you, if you don't move a little faster sirrah, or by— —I'll go and get a hickory off the pache tree and give you a damn'd cow skinning." (*Beers's Almanac for...1798*(31784))

Lord St. John being some time ago in want of a servant, an Irishman offered his service, but being asked what countryman he was? He answered an Englishman. "Where was you born?" "In Ireland, please your Lordship," said the man. "How then can you be an Englishman?" said his Lordship.___"My Lord," replied the man, " *supposing I was born in a stable, that is no reason I should be a horse.*" (*Beers's Almanac for...1798* (31784))

An American gentleman some years ago was shewing an Irishman a figure of a ship, very elegantly painted upon a wall at Haerlem, when the Hibernian, after viewing it with evident marks of delight, exclaimed, "By St. Patrick, it is mighty beautiful; I am sure it was never done in this country."—"How can that be" (said the American,) "when you see it pourtray'd upon the wall." "Arrah! and so it is" (replied the other much embarrassed at his his own want of observation), "but I mean the man who did it, never was here." (*Father Abraham's Almanac, for...1798*(32310))

In the debate on the leather tax, in the Irish House of Commons, the Chancellor of the Exchequer (Sir John Parnell) observed, with great emphasis, "That in the prosecution of this war, every man ought to give his *last* guinea to protect the remainder."

Mr. Vandelure said, "However that might be, the tax on leather would be severely felt by the *barefooted* peasantry of Ireland."

To which, Sir Boyle Roach replied, "That this could be easily remedied, by making the under *leather of wood.*" (*The Farmer's Almanack...for...1798* (32921))

Two Irishmen fighting together, one of them knocked the other down, and seeing him lie motionless, thot he had killed him; taking him, however, by the hand he cried; "O my dear Paddy, now be after speaking to me, and if I have killed you, tell me honey!" To which the other answered— "No my dear Mac, I an't dead at all, but by my shoul I am spaechless." (*The United States Almanac, for... 1799* (34547))

From an Irish Lady to her nephew

June 2, 1795

Dear Nephew,

I have not written to you since my last before now, because we have moved from our former place of living and I did not know where a letter would reach you; but I now with pleasure take my pen to inform you of the melancholy news of the death of our only living uncle Kilpatrick, who died very suddenly last week after a lingering illness of five months. The poor man was in violent convulsion the whole time of his sickness, laying perfectly quiet, and speechless, all the while talking incoherently, and calling for water. I had no opportunity of informing you of his death sooner, except I had wrote you by last post, which went off two days before he died, and then you would have had postage to pay. I am at a loss to tell what his death was occasioned by, but I fear it was brought on by his last sickness, for he was never well ten days together, during the whole time of his confinement, and I believe his sickness was occasioned by his eating too much of rabbits stuffed with peas and gravy, or peas and gravy stuffed with rabbits, I cannot tell which, but be that as it will, as soon as he breathed his last the doctor gave over all hopes of his recovery.

I need not tell you any thing about his age, for you well know that in December next, he would have been twenty-five years old lacking ten months, and had he lived till then he would have been just six months dead. His property now revolves to his next of kin, who died some time ago, so that I expect it will be divided between us, and you know his property was something very considerable, for he had a fine estate which was sold to pay his debts; and the remainder he lost in a horse race; but it was the opinion of every body at the track that he would have won the race, if the horse he ran against had not been too fast for him. I never saw a man and the doctors all say so, that observed directions and took medicine better than he did, he said he would as lives drink gruel as wine if it had only the same taste and would as soon take jalap as eat beef steak if it had the same relish. But poor soul he will never eat or drink more, and now you have not a living relative in the world except myself and your two cousins who were killed in the war. I can't dwell on this mournful subject; and shall seal my letter with black sealing wax and put on it my uncle's coat of arms, so I beg you not to break the seal when you open the letter, and don't open it till three or four days after you receive it, by which time you will be prepared for the sorrowful tidings. When you come to this place stop and do not read any more till my next.

Your affectionate Aunt

P.S. Don't write me again till you receive this. (*The American Almanac, for...1801* (36808))

A number of gentlemen dining one day upon Salmon, some of them preferring Pickerel, others Mackeral; an Irishman standing up, says, "by J——s, of all the fish in the Sea, I prefer pork and peas." (*The Farmer's Alamanac, for...1801* (36925))

B. Other Foolishness

An Irish sailor, as he was riding, made a pause—the horse in beating off the flies caught his hind foot in the stirrup; the sailor observing it said, "How now dobbin, if you are going to *get on* I'll *get off*, for d—n me if I'll ride *double with you*." (*Wheeler's North American Calendar, or an Almanack, for...1791* (23073))

An Irishman went to a Physician and desired to be inoculated. The physician complied with his request; but his inoculation did not take. He repeated the operation a second and a third time; still it did not take. "I am greatly surprised," says the Doctor. "Not so much as I am," returned the Hibernian; "for when I was inoculated twenty years ago, *it took the first time*." (*Beers's Almanac...for...1794* (25152))

Paddy finding a toad in the garden soon after his arrival, picked him up and stoking him gently, said, "A pretty bird, a pretty bird, but you've got no tail at-all at-all." (*Stoddard's Diary: or, the Columbia Almanack, for...1796* (29124))

An English and an Irishman being together at a tavern, called for a supper of bacon and eggs; when it was brought in, the Englishman said there was chickens in the eggs. "Be easy, be easy," says Paddy, "they'll make us pay the more for them." (*The New-Hampshire Diary; or Almanack: for...1797* (30857))

Two sailors, one Irish the other English, agreed reciprocally to take care of each other, in case of either's being wounded in action about to commence. It was not long before the Englishman's leg was shot off by a cannon ball; and on his calling to Paddy to carry him to the Doctor, according to their agreement, the other very readily complied; but he had scarcely got his wounded companion on his back, when a second ball struck off his head. Paddy, who through the noise and disturbance common in a sea engagement, had not perceived his friend's last misfortune, continued to make the best of his way to the Surgeon. An officer observing him with a headless trunk upon his shoulder, asked him where he was going? "To the Doctor," says Paddy. "The Doctor!" says the officer, " *why you blockhead the man has lost his head.*" On hearing this he flung the body from his shoulder, and looking at it very attentively,   " *By my shoul,*" says he, *"he told me it was his leg."* (*The New-England Almanac...for...1798* (32012))

A lady observing in company how glorious and useful a body the sun was--" *The sun to be sure,*" says an Irish gentleman present, " *is a fine body; but in my opinion, the moon is much more useful; for the moon affords us light in the night-time, when we really want it; whereas we have the sun with us on in the day-time when we have no occasion for it.*" (*The Virginia Almanac...for...1799* (33455))

Two Irishmen being one day a gunning, a large flock of pigeons came flying over their heads, when Patrick elevated his piece, and firing, brought one of them to the ground; "arra," exclaimed his companion, "what a fool you are to waste your ammunition, when the bare fall would have killed him." (*The Starry Calculator; being an Almanac for...1799* (34596))

An Englishman and an Irishman were condemned for piracy. For that crime they are generally executed near a river. The Englishman was to suffer first, but by some accident the rope slipped and he fell into the water. Being an excellent swimmer, he swam to the other side of the river and made his escape. The Irishman seeing what had happened, begged for the executioner to tie his rope fast.—"For" (says he) "if it should chance to slip, I shall certainly loose my life for I cannot swim." (*The Kentucky Almanac, for...1800* (35684))

An Irish gentleman, deranged in his mind made two attempts one morning to drown himself; but as he was an expert swimmer, in spite of his wish to die he could not help emerging from the water; therefore making to the land he tucked himself up in his garters on a neighboring tree. Soon after a party of his friends came hot foot after him and seeing him dangling in the air whilst an Irish cowkeeper was whistling, on a stile very near, unconcerned—"Why you thief," (said one of them to the fellow,) "could you be after standing there whistling and see the *jontleman* tuck himself up without offering to cut him down?"—"Arrah, pon my conscience," (says Paddy) "I was not *impartinent*: for as I saw the *jontleman* come out of the river as wet as a drowned rat, divil burn me, but I thought he had only hung himself up to dry." (*The Connecticut Pocket Almanac, for...1800* (36384))

C. Irish Belligerence

An officer in one of the Irish regiments in the French service, being dispatched by the Duke of Berwick to the King of France, with a complaint relating to some irregularities that had happened in the regiment, the King told him, his Irish troops gave him more trouble than all his forces besides.

"Sir," says the officer, "all your Majesty's enemies make the same complaint." (*Father Abraham's Almanack, for...1778* (15576))

An Irishman at an assize in Cork was arraigned for felony, before Judge Mounteney. He was asked who he would be tried be.—"By no one, by J——s!" says he. The jailer demanded him to say, "By God and his Country."—"God d—n my s—l if I do!" says Paddy, "for I don't like it at all at all, my dear." "What's that you say, honest man?" (says the Judge). "See there now" says the criminal, "his Lordship, long life to him, calls me an honest man, and why should I plead guilty?" "What do you say" (says the Judge in an authoratative voice) "I say, my Lord, I won't be tried by God at all at all, for he knows all about the matter, but I will be tried by your Lordship and my country." (*The Virginia Almanack, for...1788* (20199))

A serjeant (probably an Irishman) being on a march at the head of a company, a dog ran up at him with open mouth, to make a snap. The serjeant having a fixed bayonet ran it down the dog's throat and killed him. The owner coming up made a great outcry at his dog being killed, and demanded of the son of Mars why he could not as well have struck him with the butt end of his musquet?—" *So I would*" (answered the serjeant) " *if he had run at me with his tail end foremost.*" (*Father Abraham's Almanac, for...1798* (32310))

At Hempstead Assembly, some time since, an Irish gentleman, who danced with great spirit, though not perhaps with all the grace of a *Vestras*, was observed by a macaroni, in the same country dance, who immediately began mimicking him in the most extravagant manner. The Irishman took no notice for some time; but seeing himself the general object of laughter, he came very deliberately up to the mimic, and asked, "Why he presumed to take him off?" "Me, sir," said the other, "you mistake the matter, it is my natural way of dancing." "It is?" said the Hibernian, seemingly accepting the excuse, "well to be sure, no body can help what is natural; but, hark ye, my friend, be sure you continue in that *natural* step all night; for if you once attempt to make it *artificial*, I will break every bone in your skin." The poor macaroni was obliged to subscribe to the sentence, to the no small amusement, as well as satisfaction of the whole company. (*Hodge's North-Carolina Almanack, for . . . 1798* (32923))

An Irish gentleman lately fought a duel with his intimate friend, because he jocosely asserted that he was born without a shirt on his back. (*Beer's Almanac for . . .1801* (36924))

D. Irish thievery

A poor fellow in Dublin, some time since, was taken up for stealing a boiled leg of mutton, and was caught eating it. When he was put to the *Bar*, Lord Earhart asked of what profession he was? The Prisoner replied, "a Barrister." "Pray," continued his Lordship, "how come you to the Bar?" "In the same manner," says he, "that you did—I *eat* my way to it!" (*Beers's Almanac . . . for . . .1794* (25152))

An Irish peasant was carried before a magistrate on a charge of having stolen a sheep, the property of Garrat Fitz Maurice. The Justice asked him if he could read. "A little." "You could not be ignorant then that the sheep found in your possession belonged to Sir Garrat as his brand (GFM) was on it?" "True, . . . but I really thought the three letters stood for Good Fat Mutton." (*The Columbian Almanac . . . for . . .1796* (28450))

A dragoon was shot in Dublin for desertion, and taking away his horse and accoutrements at the same time. When on his trial, an officer asked him what could induce him to take his horse away? To which he replied, "he ran away with him"—"What," said the officer, "did you do with the money you sold him for?"—"That," please your honour," said the fellow, with the utmost indifference, "ran away too." (*The Columbian Almanac, for . . .1797* (30244))

A Countryman was indicted and arraigned for stealing a Goose; but the accusation was false; for he brought a Neighbour of his who swore, positively, that he remembered that very Goose in his possession, ever since it was a Gosling. An Irishman, who was a Prisoner for stealing a Gun, hearing this able defence, prevailed on a fellow Countryman of his to swear, that he remembered the Gun in his possession, ever since it was a *Pistol*. (*The Columbian Almanac for...1798* (31955))

E. Irish Tricksters

"Ah, honey!" (said an Irishman to his friend one day) "can you lend me ten-pence?"—"No indeed I can't" (replied Paddy) "for I have no more nor four-pence."—"Well give me that" (returned the other) "and then you'll owe me six-pence." (*An Almanack...for...1794* (25850))

A few years since, James Malone Esq. mayor of Cork, imagining that if he could strip the beggars of the miserable and sickly appearance they generally made, he should divest them of the strongest [   ] to the charity of the humane, came to the following agreement with one Geohagen, one of his constables, who was by trade a barber, viz. He directed the barber to seize all the beggars he found strolling within the limits of the city, for each of whom he promised a reward; but instead of bringing them before him (the mayor) he was to take them to his shop, and there shave, wash, dress and powder them in the [   ]est manner. He seized about half a dozen, and with the assistance of razors, wash balls, scissors, and powder puffs, he so compleatly metamorphosed them, that those who he had apprehended as mendicants, when they left his shop appeared like macaronies, at least about the head. This laughable scheme was attended with such success, that the whole tribe, during Squire Malone's mayoralty avoided his jurisdiction as carefully as if it was visited by pestilence. (*The Farmer's Almanack, for...1800* (36680))

Three Paddies having four dollars which they wished divided equally between them and seeing it was utterly impossible to divide the odd dollar, were about giving up the point: at last says one: "by St. Patric, I've hit upon it, there's two for you two and two for me too." (*The United States Almanac, for... 1801* (36934))

F. Miscellaneous Irish Stories

The boat's crew of a ship was lying in Dublin harbour, having got ashore, went soon after to their rendevoux; and one of them leaving his comrades in the house, went out upon George's Key with a tankard of porter in his hand; meeting some fellows walking along, he began to hug his pot, and accosting them, "Here is stingo," says he, "none of your damned stale Dublin ale, but porter my boys, London porter, I say, it is both meat and drink to a man." Before he had well finished his harangue, his foot slipt, and he fell down one of the stairs, or landing places; while he lay thus extended, with the water running over him, up steps one of the Irishmen, "How goes it my dear boy? You told us just now you had got both meat and drink. Now, by St. Patrick, you have also got washing and lodging." (*Father Abraham's Almanack, for . . . 1778* (15576))

A company of Gentlemen at a tavern in Pall Mall, having a mind to amuse themselves, desired the waiter to send in a chairman; it was an exceeding cold night in the month of December, and when the chairman, who chanced to be an Irishman, came in, one of the company asked him, with a very grave face, how much he would take to go naked to the top of St. Pauls. Paddy, shrugging up his shoulders, said, "Arrah, Sir, you are certainly joking now; what would I take! by St. Patrick, Gentlemen, I'd take my death of cold." (*Bickerstaff's New-England Almanack, for . . . 1780* (16672))

An Irishman, who was a genuine Paddy, called on Col. Lyon, and desired to be employed as a workman in his Forge; the Colonel waited on his countryman to view his works; on their way they met with one of those animals which generally make their abode in and about ponds; the Hibernian having never seen the like, asked the Colonel what it was; who answered a Turtle; "a Durkee," said the Paddy, "and can he fly?" At the same time pointing toward it his national Club, on which Mr. Amphibious (as is usual for them) drew his head back immediately into the shell; on which the Paddy, in surprise, exclaimed, "J——s, see how he swallows his head." (*The Virginia Almanack, for . . . 1794* (25112))

A young lady who visited Portsmouth this week declares, that the Irish gentlemen are the politest she ever met with; as a gentleman of that nation, notwithstanding the scarcity of *beds* in that town, offered her part of his *own*. (*The United States Almanac . . . for . . . 1797* (30437))

Captain N. who lately arrived at Boston, when going to the wharf, ordered an Irishman to throw over the bouy, and going below for a few minutes he called to his Irish servant and asked him if he had thrown over the bouy!—"No, sir," says he, "indeed I could not catch the boy, but I threw over the old cook!" (*The United States Almanac, for . . . 1799* (34546))

An Irishman was lately brought before a Justice, charged with marrying six wives. The Magistrate asked him, how he could be so hardened a villain? "Please your worship," says paddy, " *I was trying to get a good one.*" (*Isaiah Thomas's Massachusetts, Connecticut, Rhodeisland, Newhampshire & Vermont Almanac . . . for . . . 1799* (34562))

An Irish fortune hunter, at——, telling Dr. Smollet that he had got an excellent phaeton, on a new plan: "I am rather of opinion," says the Doctor, "that you have got it on the *old plan*; for I suppose you *never meant to pay for it*." (*The Farmer's Almanack, for...1800* (36680))

An Irishman boasting that he was owner of a large farm which he said he had left in Ireland was asked the cause of his leaving so valuable an estate to come to this country where he had no possessions? "Ah!" says Paddy, "it was indeed under a small incumbrance; for another man's land lay right a top of it." (*Beers's Almanac for...1801* (36924))

An Irishman fell from the main top of a ship, on the main deck near the first lieutenant. Everyone thought his bones were broken; he at last got up and rubbed his arm, the officer asked from whence he came! *" Please your honor*," said he, *" I'm from the North of Ireland*." (*Lilly's Almanac for...1801* (37829))

BLACKS

A. Blacks as Noble Savages

A Negro, Quashi, was accused and to be whipped for a crime he was innocent of. He escaped and threw down his master and while holding him said, "Master, I was bred up with you from a child: I was your playmate when a boy: I have loved you as myself: your interest has been my study: I am innocent of the cause of your suspicion: had I been guilty, my attachment to you might have pleaded for me; yet you have condemned me to a punishment of which I must ever have borne the disgraceful mark—thus only can I avoid them." With these words, he drew his knife with all his strength across his own throat, and fell down dead, without a groan, on his master, bathing him in his blood. (*The Columbian Almanack, for...1791* (22411))

In the most flourishing period of the reign of Louis XIV, two negro youths, the sons of a prince, being brought to the court of France, the King appointed a Jesuit to instruct them in letters, and in the Christian religion; and gave to each of them a commission in his guards. The elder, who was remarkable for his candour and ingenuity, made great improvements, more particularly in the doctrines of religion. A brutal officer upon some dispute, insulted him with a blow. The gallant youth never so much as offered to resent it. A person who was his friend, took an opportunity to talk with him that evening alone upon his behaviour, which he told him was too tame, especially in a soldier. "Is there, then," said the young African, "one revelation for soldiers, and another for merchants and gownmen? The good father, to whom I owe all my knowledge, has earnestly inculcated forgiveness of injuries to me; assuring me, that a Christian was by no means to retaliate abuses of any kind." "The good father," replied his friend, "may fit you for a monastery by his lessons, but never for an army and the rules of a court. In a word," continued he, "if you do not call the colonel to account, you will be branded with an infamy of cowardice, and have your commission taken from you." "I would fain," answered the young man, "act consistently in every thing; but since you press me with that regard to my honour which you have always shewn, I will wipe off so foul a stain; though I must own I gloried in it before." Immediately upon this, he desired his friend to go from him and appoint the aggressor to meet him early in the morning. Accordingly they met and fought; and the brave youth disarmed his adversary, and forced him to ask his pardon publically. This done, the next day he threw up his commission and desired the king's leave to return to his father. At parting, he embraced his brother and his friend, with tears in his eyes, saying, He did not imagine the Christians had been such unaccountable people; and that he could not apprehend their faith was of any use to them, if it did not influence their practice. "In my country we think it is no dishonour to act according to the principles of our religion." (*The Philadelphia Almanac, for...1800* (35728))

B. Blacks as Fools

"It is a very dark night," said Cato to one of his brethren of colour, as they were both staggering home from a frolic on a thanksgiving eve— Staggering, did I say?—They were not drunk, nor were they sober: They were at that happy medium, when the bondsman feels himself as happy as the Monarch.

"It is a very dark night, Cesar; take care," said Cato. The caution was a good one; but, like many others, was given too late: For Cesar, striking his foot against the small remains of a post which Time had been hacking to pieces, measured his length upon the ground, before the friendly caution of Cato had met his ear. "I wonder," said Cesar, rising and rubbing the mud &c. from his holiday suit, "why de Dible de Sun no shine in dese dark nights, Cato; and not keep shining in de day time, when dere's no need of him." (*The United States Almanac...for...1798* (33101))

In the time of the religious awakening produced by the popular Whitefield, two negroes were resolved to be converted. [Here the copy is extremely poor. They apparently attend a service, see a preacher and begin to show their enthusiasm by weeping, shouting and] soon rolled themselves in spiritual agony on the ground. In the course of their pious revolutions they chanced to roll into a cow t—d. Upon being told, at length, that it was not Mr. Whitefield, they sprang up with exclaiming, "Garra dam my soul! not Massa Whiterfed? den y' sea we besha—ourself for no ting." (*The Farmer's Almanack, for...1800*

A gentleman lately riding from Hanover to Pompton, being a stranger to the way, enquired of an African, who readily gave him the following directions verbatim—"Why Masser you must keep right e long. I don't know da be any wrong road you be like to miss, ceptin de right one; so I don't see how you can possibly get out de way." (*The United States Almanac, for... 1801* (36934))

A captain of a ship, having a Negro pilot on board, in crossing Charleston bar, asked him what water the ship was in? "Salt water, massa." "I know that," replied the captain, "but how much water is there?" "Ah, massa, you tink me bring tin pot for measure um?" (*Curtis's Pocket Almanack, for... 1801* (37275))

Not long since a negro fellow, by the name of Primus, being arraigned before a justice of the peace (who has lately resigned) for trial, was questioned in the following manner.—"Primus, what is your plea, guilty or not guilty?" "I don't know, Massa," said Primus, "dat be for de court to determine." (*The New-England Almanack for... 1801* (37279))

C. Blacks as Slaves

A Negro fellow being strongly suspected of having stolen goods in his possession, was taken before a certain justice of peace in Philadelphia, and charged with the offence. The fellow acknowledged the fact, and made the following speech, "Massa Justice, me know me got dem tings from Tom dere, and me tinke Tom teal dem too, but what den, Massa? dey be only a picaninny corkscrew and a picaninny knife; one cost sixpence and tudda a shilling; and me pay Tom for dem honestly Massa." "A very pretty story, truly; you knew they were stolen, and yet alledge in excuse you paid honestly for them, I'll teach you better law than that sirrah! don't you know, Caesar, the receiver is as bad as the thief? You must be severely whipt you black rascal, you!"

"Very well, Massa? If de black rascal be whipt for buying tolen goods, me hope de white rascal be wipt too for same ting, when me catch him, as well as Caesar." "To be sure," rejoined his worship. "Well den," says Caesar, "here be Tom's massa, hold him fast constable, he buy Tom as I buy picaninny knife and picaninny corkscrew. He know every well poor Tom be tolen from his fadder and mudder; de knife and de corkscrew have neder."

Whether it was that his worship, as well as Tom's master, were smote in the same instant with the justice or severity of Caesar's application, we know not; but after a few minutes pause, Caesar was dismissed, and the action discharged. (*Bickerstaff's Genuine Almanack, for . . . 1791* (23069))

During the late war a certain planter on the north side of Jamaica (remarkable for starving his negroes) frequently scanted them in their weekly allowance of herrings and Indian meal. The Negroes more than once came in a body and demanded the reason why they were thus stinted in the article of food? The constant reply from their master, manager or overseer was, "Boys, the provision vessels were all taken by the American privateers!" This answer in some measure satisfied the slaves for several months; at length, upon a constant repetition thereof, and being exhausted with continual fasting, one of the principal negroes, in the name of the rest, proposed the following question—"Massa, de provisions taken ebery day by the Merican pribateer, vy not too take de vessel wid de grubbin hoe and de pick-axe?" (*The Virginia Almanack, for . . . 1792* (23125))

A Negro who had a cruel master was asked if the son was *a chip of the old block.* "No, no," says Pompey, "young massa *all block.*" (*Wheeler's North-American Calendar, for . . . 1793* (25027))

A traveller relates, that being with a party of friends caught in bad weather upon one of the West-India islands, he took shelter at the public house, kept by a foreigner: upon their desiring, that more wood might be brought to the fire, the brute ordered his sickly wife to go forth into the storm, and fetch it! while a young sturdy negro wench, his slave, stood by doing nothing! Upon being asked why he did not send the girl rather than his wife? he replied, "that wench is worth 80 pounds and if she should catch cold and die, it would be a great loss to me; but if my wife dies, I can get another, and perhaps money in the bargain." (*The Virginia Almanac, for . . . 1799* (34943))

An old gentleman at the point of death, called a faithful negro to him, telling him he would do him an honour before he died. The fellow thanked him and hopped massa would live long. "I intend, Cato," said the master, "to allow you to be buried in the family vault." "Ah master," returns Cato, "me no like dat, ten pounds would be better to Cato. he no care where he be buried, besides massa, suppose we be buried togeder, and de devil come looking for massa in the dark, he might take away poor negar man in mistake." (*Weatherwise's Massachusetts, Connecticut, Rhodeisland, Newhampshire and Vermont Almanack, for . . . 1799* (34969))

D. Blacks As Tricksters

A clergyman in New jersey owned a negro by the name of Quash who was by no means fond of working, and one day told his master he conceived it a great hardship, "dat the poor negar man mus worke so hard, and massa do noting." "You are mistaken, Quash, my labour is more fatiguing than your's; I do head work and yours is mere bodily excercise." This hint was sufficient for Quash. The next day he was ordered into the woods to procure fuel; but Quash staying longer than usual, the parson repaired to the woods to see what detained him; when behold; the first object that presented itself to his view was Quash astride on a large maple-log, in a pensive attitude. When he enquired the cause, Quash started up and rubbing his midnight brow, "Oh massa, me—me have been doing head work." "Well, let me hear what your head has done." "Suppose, massa, dere be five pidgeons on dis tree, and you take a gun and shoot two of them, how many dere be left?" "Why, three, you old sinner." "No, massa, *dem toder tree fly away.*" (*Beers's Almanac...for...1797* (30044))

A gentleman in the state of Connecticut, regularly attended public worship on the Lord's day, with all his family: On the Sabbath evening he always catachised his children and servants on the principles of religion and what they heard the minister deliver from the pulpit. He had a negro man who never could remember a note of the sermon, though otherwise smart. At last his master peremptorily told him, he would Monday morning tie him up and flog him. Next Sabbath evening, when interrogated, he had forgotten all: On Monday morning his master executes his threats so far, as to tie him up. The fellow then cried out, "O master spare me, for I remember something the minister said." "What is it," said the master. The fellow replied. " *This much may suffice at this time.*" His master was so pleased with his wit, that he forgave him. (*Beers's Almanac for...1798* (31784))

Two negroes meeting in a dram shop, called for a bowl of grog— after it was made, one fellow takes up the bowl, and after drinking two thirds of the contents, cries "Hem! hem! Massa dis here too trong: *do put little more water here.*" "Tay, mate," says the other one: "no be in sitch dam hurre: *let me cry hem too.*" (*The Farmer's Calendar; or, Fry and Southwick's Almanack, for...1798* (33172))

E. Repartee of Blacks

A Negro servant being asked what colour he believed the devil was? "Why," replied the African, "the white men paint him *black*, we say he is *white*; but from his great age, and being called *Old Nick*, I should suppose him *grey*. (*Wheeler's North American Calendar, or an Almanack, for...1791* (23073))

A zealous clergyman had taken for his text these words, "And Satan came also among them" at the moment of his reading the text an old decrepit Negro entering the sanctuary supposed himself pointed at, and with a degree of resentment, looked the priest full in the face—"You grad to see your fader?" (*The Virginia Almanack, for...1796* (28197))

A minister being possessed of a wench to whom a certain negro man made his addresses: The parson having some objections which he made to the poor black, who, not liking the opposition to his courtship took the liberty to ask him a question, viz. " *Masar no wat the elebenth commanment be?*" The poor parson could not tell,—" *Well,*" says the negro, "me tell what it be: De elebenth commandment is, BES WAY EVERYONE MINE HE OWN BUSINESS." (*The Columbian Almanac for...1796* (28784))

A very pious gentleman, but rather worldly, who lives not a thousand miles from Boston, made it his constant practice to call up his family before day, in order to attend prayers and be ready for their labours in good season; one morning, having mustered his family rather earlier than common, he commenced family duties by prayer, during which, he returned thanks to the Lord that they were brought to see the light of another day—an old negro standing by, cries out, "Top, top, vass a bit, no day yet, massa, certain—no day yet." (*An Astronomical Diary, or Almanack, for...1796* (29493))

True African Wit

Old Cato, on his death bed lying,
Worn out with work and almost dying,
With patience heard his friends propose,
What bearers for him they had chose.
"There's Cuff and Caesar; Pomp and Plato,
Will they do?" "bery well." quoth Cato,
"And Baalum Philips, now for t'other
We must take Scipio, Baalum's brother.
I no like Scip," old Cato cries
"Scip rascal, tell about me lies,
And get me whipt."—"Well! is all one,
Scip shall be bearer, Scip, or none."

"Mind me," cried Cato, "if dat cur,
Dat Scip comes bearer, I won't die!"
(*The Calendar of Maine or Eastern Almanack for...1797* (30699))

It is well known that the name Nicholas has been generally abbreviated into Nick. An old Negro, named Harry, who lived in Newjersey some years ago, commonly made it his practice on Hollidays, to go round among the Gentry, begging. One Christmas morning, meeting Mr. Nicholas G. he thus accosted him; "Good morning, Massa G. wish you melly Clismus: Please to gib poor old Negur six pence dis morning?" Mr. G. who well knew the Negro, but determined to have a little fun, replied with some degree of sterness, "Who are you?" "Massa no know me?" (answered the Negro) "My name Harry: Dey call me Ole Harry." "Old Harry!" (said Mr. G.) "they call the Devil Old Harry." "Yes, Massa," (replied the Negro) "sometime Ole Harry, sometime Ole Nick." Mr. G. was so pleased with the repartee, that he gave the Negro a dollar. (*Dickson's Balloon Almanac, for...1799* (33636))

A man passing in the road after a horse, which had run away from him, enquired, in a passion, of a negro wench, whether she had seen him, observing, he believed he had gone to the *Devil*. "If that be the case," she replied, "you need not give yourself any trouble, keep on your way, and you will *certainly* overtake him." (*An Astronomical Diary, or Almanac, for...1799* (34529))

A negro fiddler making his brags to a minister on the great sum he had procured by his practice asked him if it was not equal to his salary and being told it was says, "Well massa, I pose I sute de hearers good eal better." (*Beers's Almanac for...1801* (36924))

F. Miscellaneous Stories about Blacks

Sir William Gooch being in conversation with a gentleman in a street of the city of Williamsburg, returned the salute of a negro, who was passing by about his master's business.

"Sir," said the gentleman, "does your honor descend so low as to salute a slave?"

"Why," replied the governor, "Yes: I cannot suffer a man of his condition to exceed me in good manners." (*Bickerstaff's New-England Almanack for...1776* (14066))

A young gentleman by the name of Lord, went to pay a lady a visit one evening, and being a novice in the business, and bashful withal, was rather backward in doing his errand. It growing somewhat late, she asked him whether he wished to go to bed; and on his concluding to go, though with great reluctance, she conducted him into a back [ ] where a negro (who happened to be gone) usually slept, and left him to his repose. Toward morning, the old negro returned, and finding his bed occupied, demanded who was there? and being answered "Lord" he exclaimed, "Lord, God or de dibble, he no bisnes here;" and packt him off. (*The Farmer's Almanac, for...1800* (35167))

Account of a Wonderful talent for arithmatical calculation, in an African slave, living in Virginia.

There is now living about four miles from Alexandria, in the state of Virginia, a negro slave of seventy years old, of the name of Thomas Fuller, the property of Mrs. Elizabeth Coxe. This man possesses a talent for arithmetical calculations, the history of which, I conceive merits a place in the records of the human mind. He is a native of Africa, and can neither read nor write. Two natives of Pennsylvania, viz. William Hartshorn and Samuel Coates, men of property and respectable characters, having heard in traveling through the neighborhood in which the slave lived, of his extraordinary powers in arithmetic, sent for him, and had their curiosity sufficiently gratified by the answers which he gave to the following questions.

First: upon being asked how many seconds there are in a year and a half, he answered in about two minutes, 47,304,000. Second, on being asked, how many seconds a man has lived who is seventeen years, fifteen days, and twelve hours old, he answered in a minute and a half 2,216,500,800.

One of the gentlemen, who employed himself with [paper   ] in making these calculations, told him he was wrong and that the sum was not so great as he had said, upon which the African hastily replied, " 'top, massa, you forget de leap year." On adding the seconds of the leap year to the others, the amount of the whole in both their sums agreed exactly.

Third. The following question was then proposed to him: suppose a farmer has six sows, and each sow has six female pigs the first year, and they increase in the same proportion, to the end of eight years, how many sows will the farmer then have? In ten minutes, he answered [13,772,858]. The difference of time between his answering this and the two former questions was made by a trifling mistake he made from a misapprehension of the question.

In the presence of Thomas Wistor and Benjamin Morris two respectable citizens of Philadelphia, he gave the amount of nine figures multiplied by nine.

He informed the first mentioned gentlemen that he began his application to figures by counting ten, and that when he was able to count to a hundred he thought himself (to use his own words) "a very clever fellow.'

His first attempt after this was to count the number of hairs in a cows tail, which he found to be 2872.

He next amused himself with counting, grain by grain, a bushel of wheat and a bushel of flax seed.

From this he was led to calculate with the most perfect accuracy, how many shingles a house of certain dimensions would require to cover it, and how many grains of corn were necessary to sow a certain quantity of ground.

From this application of his talents, his mistress has often derived considerable benefit.

At the time he gave account of himself, he said his memory began to fail him—he was grey headed, and exhibited several other marks of the weakness of old age—he had worked hard upon a farm during the whole of his life, but had never been intemperate in the use of spirituous liquors. He spoke with great respect of his mistress, and mentioned in a particular manner his obligation to her for refusing to sell hem, which she had been tempted to do by offers of large sums of money, from several curious persons.

One of the gentlemen (Mr. Coats) having remarked in his presence, that it was a pity he had not had an education equal to his genius; he said "no massa—it is best I got no learning; for many learned men be great fools." (*The Columbian Almanack...for...1791* (22411))

AMERICAN INDIANS

A. Indians as Cruel and Degraded Savages

Some years ago, the Shawano Indians being obliged to remove from their habitations, in the way took a Muskohga warrior, known by the name of Old Serarar, prisoner. They bastinadoed him severely, and condemned him to the fiery torture: he underwent a great deal without showing any concern; his countenance and behavior were as if he suffered not the least pain. He told his persecutors with a bold voice, that he was a warrior; that he gained the most of his martial reputation at the expense of their nation, and was desirous of shewing them in the act of dying, that he was still as much their superior as when he headed his gallant countrymen against them; that although he had fallen into their hands, and had forfeited the protection of the Divine Power by some impiety or other, when carrying the holy ark of war against his devoted enemies, yet he had so much remaining virtue as would enable him to punish himself more exquisitely than all their despicably ignorant crowd could do, if they would give him liberty by untying him and handing him one of the red hot gun barrels out of the fire. The proposal, and his method of address appearing so exceedingly bold and uncommon, that his request was granted. Then suddenly seizing one end of the red hot barrel, and brandishing it from side to side, forced his way through the armed and surprised multitude, leaped down a prodigious steep and high bank, into a branch of the river, dived through it, ran over a small island, and passed the other branch amidst a shower of bullets; and though numbers of his enemies were in close pursuit of him, he got into a bramble swamp, through which, though naked and in a mangled condition, he reached his own country. (*The Columbian Almanac: or, the North American Calendar, for...1793* (24202))

An Indian chief being asked his opinion of a cask of Madeira wine presented to him by an officer, said he thought it a juice extracted from women's tongues and lion's hearts; for after he had drank a bottle of it, he said, he could talk for ever and fight the devil. (*Beer's Almanac for...1794* (25152))

An Indian who was appointed a Justice of Peace, issued the following warrant.—"Me High Howder, yu constable, yu deputy, best way you' look um Jeremiah Wicket, strong yu take um, fast yu hold um, quick yu bring um before me."

Captain Howder"

(*The New England Almanac...for...1798* (32012))

Of all the vices incident to the aboriginals of this country, that of lying is not the least. Some years since one Tom Hyde, an Indian famous for his cunning came into a tavern at Brookfield, and after a little talk told the landlord he had been hunting, and had killed a fine fat deer, and that if he would give him a quart of rum, he would tell him where it was. The landlord did not wish to let slip so good an opportunity to attain his venison, and immediately measured the Indian his rum—"Well," says Tom, "do you know where the great meadow is?"—"Yes"—"Well, do you know the great marked maple tree, that stands in it?"—"Yes."—"Well, there lies the deer," Away posted the taverner, with his team, in quest of his purchase, he found the meadow, and the tree, it is true; but his searchings after the deer were in vain, and he returned no heavier, (but in chagrin) than he went. Some days after he meets the Indian, and violently accuses him of the deception.—Tom heard him out, and, with the coolness of a philosopher, replied, "Did you not find the meadow, as I said?" "Yes." "And the tree?" "Yes."—"And the deer?" "No." "Very good," continues he, "you found two truths to one lie, which was very well for an Indian."

(*Franklin's Legacy: or, The New-York and Vermont Almanack, for...1799* (34376))

A reasonable quantity of money is so necessary to the comfort of life, that we ought to be careful in its expenditure, that we may not only have enough for ordinary purposes, but a little stock beyond this for extraordinary contingencies. We ought to think like the Indian, who, being asked what three things he would wish to possess, if in his power, answered, "as much rum as I can drink—a fine squaw"—and, being at a loss for the third, at last said, "hang it! I will have a little more rum." We should endeavor to have money enough—and a little more money for an uncommon emergence. (*An Astronomical Diary, or Almanac, for...1799* (34529))

A clergyman who had lately been preaching among the Indians, being in conversation with one of his brother preachers, observed to him, that he believed his was the means of sending many a poor savage to Abraham's bosom. "If he did not like them better than I do," replied the other, "he would *pull out his straps and let them go.*" (*The Farmer's Almanack, for...1799* (34968))

A clergyman took for his text the following words—" *Vow and pay unto the Lord thy vows.*" An Indian heard him very attentively, and stepping up to the parson, thus accosted him. "I *vow* I'll go home with you, Mr. Minister."—"You must go then," replied the parson. The Indian afterwards *vowed* to have supper, and then to stay the night. "You may," replied the clergyman, "but I *vow* you shall go in the morning." (*Stoddard's Diary: or, the Columbia Almanack, for...1800* (35173))

B. Indian Customs

One Indian happened to kill another. The brother of the deceased called upon the murderer, and seeing a woman and children...[granted a reprieve]. As soon as the murderer's oldest son killed a deer, the brother returned. The murderer said he was ready to die, and thanked the other for so long a delay; on which the wife and children broke into tears. The murderer reproved them, and particularly his son—saying to him, "did you shed tears when you killed the deer? and if you saw him die with dry eyes, why do you weep for me, who am willing to suffer what the custom of our nation renders necessary?" With undaunted countenance he then called on the brother of the deceased to strike: and he died without a groan. (*An Almanack for...1796* (28170))

An Indian whose squaw was drowned, thus expressed his grief with true savage insensibility:—"I feel so sorry, that I could lie down and go to sleep *anywhere.*" (*Beers's Almanac for...1800* (35164))

C. Indians and Christians

In a journey to the Shawanese Indians, allies and dependants of the six nations, and some other neighbouring tribes, Mr. Sergeant offered to instruct them in the Christian religion; this however, they rejected with the utmost disdain. They even reproached Christianity; told him that the traders would, "lie, cheat and debauch their young women, and even their wives when their husbands were from home," and added that the Senecas had given them their country to live in, but had expressly charged them never to receive Christianity from the English. (*An Astronomical Diary. . .for . . .1793* (24826))

A young Indian missionary, at a catachetical lecture, demanded of a tawny princess, "How many commands there were?—" "Nine, sir," "What! have not I learnt you ten?" "Yes, Mr. Minister, and last night you *learnt me to break one.*" (*Curtis's Pocket Almanack for...1800* (35366))

A Swedish minister took occasion to inform the Chiefs of the Susquehanna Indians, in a kind of sermon, of the principal historical facts on which the Christian religion is founded; and particularly the fall of our first parents by eating an apple. When the sermon was over, an old Indian orator replied,—"What you have told us is very good; we thank you for coming so far to tell us these things you have heard from your mothers; in return we will tell you what we have heard from ours."

"In the beginning we had only flesh of animals to eat; and if they failed we starved. Two of our hunters having killed a deer, and broiled part of it, saw a young woman descend from the clouds, and seat herself on a hill hard by. Said one to the other, 'It is a spirit, perhaps, that has smelt our venison, let us offer some of it to her.' They accordingly gave her the tongue; she was pleased with its flavor, and said, 'Your kindness shall be rewarded; come here thirteen moons hence, and you shall find it.'— They did so; and found, where her right hand had touched the ground, maize growing; where her left hand had been, kidney beans; and where her back side had been, they found tobacco."

The Swedish minister was disgusted. "What I told you," said he, "is sacred truth. Yours is fable, fiction and false hood." The Indian, offended in his turn, replied, "My friend, your education has not been a good one; your mothers have not done you justice; they have not well instructed you in the rules of common civility. You saw that we, who understand and practice all these rules, believed your stories; why then do you refuse to believe ours? We believe, indeed as you have told us, that it is bad to eat apples; it had been better that they had been made into cyder; but we would not have told you so had you not disbelieved the method by which we first obtained maize, kidney beans and tobacco." (*Beer's Almanac...for...1795* (26632))

D. Other American Indian Stories

One of the aborigines of this country having a wife who often used her tongue more than he thought needful, undertook, after receiving a terrible peal from the noisy member, to exercise a little of the discipline of the rod upon her. A good Priest passing by, and hearing the fray, stopped and attempted to pacify the enraged husband, telling him he ought not to whip the woman as she was the *weaker vessel.*—"D—n her," said the Indian, "then let her carry less sail." (*Beers's Almanac...for...1794* (25152))

When general Lincoln went to make peace with the Creek Indians, one of the Chiefs asked him to sit down on a log. It was not long before he was desired to move, and in a few moments to proceed, and the request was repeated, till he found himself at the end of the log. The request was then renewed, to which he made answer, he could move no farther. "Just so it is with us," answered the tawney chief, "You have moved us back to the sea, and now ask us to go farther." (*The Columbian Almanac, for...1797* (30244))

An old American savage being at an inn in New York, met with a gentleman who gave him some liquor and being rather lively, boasted he could read and write English. The gentleman, willing to indulge him in displaying his knowledge, begged leave to propose a question, to which the old man consented. He was then asked who was the first circumcised? The Indian immediately answered, "Father Abraham:" and directly asked the gentleman, "who was the first quaker?" He said it was very uncertain as people differed in their sentiments exceedingly. The Indian perceiving the gentleman unable to resolve the question, put his fingers into his mouth to express his surprise, and looking steadfastly, told him that Mordecai was the first quaker for he would not pull off his hat to Haman. (*The Columbian Almanac: or, the North-American Calendar for...1801* (37206))

OTHER MINORITIES

A. Dutch and Germans

A poor woman applied to Hoffman, who is a German and a Chymist at Cambridge, for his advice for her husband, who was very ill. After having heard her story, Hoffman bid her get some pouppies heads, boil them in some milk, and give it to her husband. The next market day the woman came and told him her husband was not a bit better. "No," says Hoffman, "did you give him what I told you!" "O la! yes, but I was never so troubled in my life as I was to get the Puppies heads." "Good Got," says Hoffman, "I did not mean the *Pouppy dog, but Pouppy of the field.*" (*Ames' Almanack for...1792* (23121))

It is said, tho' perhaps by Way of Joke that the vulgar Dutch address their sweethearts in these Words: ["My beute Cabalauw"] that is "My dear Codfish," when they would express exceeding Fondness and Passion. (*An Astronomical Diary... for...1793* (24827))

Two eminent Dutch farmers in the township of Pequanack, in the county of Morris, known by the name of *Skin* and *Bones*, having an expectation of a scarcity of grain, made a reserve to themselves of all their crops of corn for some years past, to extort on the poor people. But the people, being much enraged at such an extortionate oppression that some of them set up a number of advertisements in the following words:
There's *Bone* and *Skin*
    Two farmers thin
To starve us all they swear it,
    But be it known
To Skin and Bone,
    That Flesh and Blood won't bare it.
(*An Astronomical Diary, or Almanack, for...1796* (29493))

Advertisement:
Yan away from mine house, more as tree weeks hence, on Pluck Horses' Stone Colt, pranded on the left off shoulter behint on the ty mit an white stripe up his forehead, like our Honesses mare: more as dat, he is the highness of the tird button of you Comisole; more as dat, be baces as hell; more as dat, I blove he has gon up Long Island, New-England, Duches County; more as dat, you pick him up, you bring him up top mine house, I make forty scallings up your pockets.
                                                                HENRY CLUNK
(*Webster's Calendar; or the Albany Almanack, for...1797* (31617))

A Dutchman and his wife were travelling; they sat down by the road exceedingly fatigued. The wife sighed—" *I wish I was in heaven*"—

The husband replied "I wish I was at the tavern." "Oh, you old rogue," says the wife, "you always want to get the best place."
(*The American Almanac for. . .1799* (33431))

An Englishman and a Dutchman disputing about the goodness of their different countries: says the Dutchman, "Your country thinks of nothing but gutting, and even the names of your places have a reference to it, you have your Portsmouths, you Plymouths, your Yarmouths, your Falmouths, your Dartmouths, your Exmouths; and you are all mouths together." "Ay," replies the Englishman, "and you have your Amster-dams, and your Roter-dams—and G. d—n you all together, say I." (*The Farmer's Almanack, for. . .1799* (33709))

B. Welchmen

Tom Dorbell meeting with a Welchman demanded his money, who answered, "Hur has no money of hur own, but has sixty pounds of hur masters, which hur can't part with"—quoth Tom, "you shan't can't me off so, for money I want and money I will have"—Whereupon the Welchman gave him his money, but being concerned how he should account with his master, says to Tom, "Pray shoot hur through hur coat so that hur master might be convinced that hur was robbed," Which Tom did accordingly. "Cuts splutter hur nails," (quoth the Welchman) "that was a fine *pounce*, pray give hur another *pounce* for hur money," which he did;—"By St. Davis," (says the Welchman) "this is a better *pounce* than t'other; pray give hur one more *pounce*." Quoth Tom, "I have no more"—"Then," says the Welchman, "but hur has one *pounce* left for hur, and if hur won't give hur back hur money, hur will pounce hur guts out;" upon which Tom delivered back the money, and so made the bargain even. (*The Connecticut Almanack, for. . .1780* (16538))

The Bad Bargain on Bothe Sides

Two Welshmen, partners in a Cow,
Resolved to sell her dear;
And laid their heads together how
To do't at Ludlow Fair.

It was a sultry summer's day,
When out they drove the beast;
And having got about half way,
They set them down to rest.

The Cow, a creature of no breeding,
(The Place with grass being stor'd)
Fed by; and while she was a feeding
Let fall a mighty t___.

"Roger," quoth Hugh, "I tell thee what,
Two words and I have done;
If thou wilt fairly eat up that,
This cow is all thy own."

" 'Tis done," quoth Roger," 'tis agreed;"
And to't went apace
He seem'd so eager, it is said,
That he forgot his grace.

He laboured with his wooden spoon,
And up he slop't the stuff,
Till by the time that half was done
He felt he had enough

He felt, but scorning to look back,
Would look as if he wanted more;
And seem'd to make a fresh attack
With as much vigour as before.

But stopping short a while, he cry'd
"How far'st thou neighbour Hugh?
I hope by this you're satisfied
Who's master of the cow."

"Ay, ay," quoth Hugh, "(the devil choke thee,
For nothing else can do't)
I'm satisfied that thou hast broke me,
Unless thou wilt give out."

"Give out," quoth Roger, "that were fine,
Why what have I been doing?
But yet I tell thee friend of mine,
I shall not seek thy ruin."

"My heart now turns against such gains—
I know thou'rt piteous poor;

> Eat then the half that still remains,
> And 'tis as was before.''

> "God's blessing on thy heart," quoth Hugh,
> That proffer none can gainsay!"
> With that he readily fell to,
> And eat his share o' the 'tansy.

> Quoth Hodge, "We're even now no doubt,
> And neither side no winner:"
> "So had we been," quoth Hugh, "without
> This dam'd confounded dinner."
> (*The York, Cumberland and Lincoln Almanack, for . . . 1788* (20467))

A young Welchman, who sometime since emigrated to this county from the Western and less cultivated parts of Wales, being withal very ignorant, and lounging one day in a grocer's store where he had no business, the grocer happened to be waited on by a person belonging to a certain bank, with what is called a bank notice— "And goot my friend," (cried Taffy) "what paper may that be now?" The grocer answered drily, "Why, it is a notice to me to prepare myself to be hang'd." "To be hanged," (said the other springing up from the counter) "why, do they send people notices before they take them to be hanged?" "Yes," replied the grocer, "God be thanked, we live in a free country and under a free government; and when it takes a notion to hang any body, it gives him three days previous notice, in order to go about town and settle his worldly affairs." The grocer soon after managed matters so as to have the bank notice slipt into the young man's hand; and next day espied him with his budget hastily stepping into a country boat. "What's the hurry—what's the hurry?" (said he)—"D—n the gallows notices" (answered Taffy;) "I have no affairs, Got be thanked, to settle here, and will get out from among you as soon as possible."
(*The United States Almanac, for . . . 1799* (34546))

C. French

A Frenchman, who spoke very broken English, having some words with his Wife, endeavored to call her *Bitch*, but could not recollect the Name; at last he thought he had done it, by saying, " *Begar, mine Deare, but you be one damn'd Dog's wife.*" "Aye, that's true enough," answered the woman, "the more's my misfortune." (*Hutchins Improved . . . for . . . 1781* (16807))

A Frenchman being taken prisoner by the Algerines was asked what he could do as a slave? His answer was, he had been used to sedentary employment. "Well then," (said the pirates) "we will put you on a pair of feather breeches, and make you hatch chickens."(*The American Almanac, for...1801* (36808))

A Frenchman very politely observed to an Englishman, that the French were the first inventors of that beautiful ornament, the Ruffle; which the Englishman readily acknowledged, mean time observing, that the English had made some little improvement by adding the shirt.

It is modestly suggested by some real friends to government, that as much improvement might be made to the American *Cockade,* if the *Spirited* wearers would equip themselves with a good gun, bayonet, &c. and learn the use of them, as there was to the Ruffle by adding a shirt. (*An Astronomical Diary, or Almanac, for...1799* (34529))

A fashionable emigrant was invited, some time since, to dine with a London Alderman, in whose hands he had lodged a sum of money, and was, for a long time tormented with extravagant encomiums on a Gibbet Pie, which his Host was most voraciously devouring. "Have you ever, Monsieur," (said Mr. Greenfat) "have you ever seen any thing like it?" "Nothing in my life" (replied the other) "except your Worship's Wig." "Ha, ha!" (exclaimed the Alderman) "that's a good one. But pray how is my Wig like that Pie?" "Par Dieu" (rejoined the Frenchman) "because it has a Goose's head in it."
(Dickson's Balloon Almanac, for...1799 (33636))

D. Jews

John, King of England, demanded a thousand marks of silver of a Jew who lived at Bristol, and on his refusal, ordered one of the Jew's teeth to be drawn every day until he should consent to pay the money; the Jew lost seven of his teeth before he would comply with the demand of the tyrant. (*Thomas's Massachusetts, New-Hampshire and Connecticut Alamanack for...1780* (16288))

The Prince of Guimeve seeing a man with a tattered pair of breeches coming into his wife's apartment, asked Madam de Guimeve, what he came to do there?

"He teaches me Hebrew," said she.

"Madam," replied M. de Guimeve, "he will soon teach you to see his backside."
(*Father Abraham's Almanack for...1779* (16050))

One day a *Jew* broker told Dr. Chovet (who affected to give no credit to accounts of the misfortunes of the British during the war) that Lord Cornwallis had been taken—and asked him, with an air of triumph, did he " *believe dat?*" "Go you *unbelieving* rascal," replies the doctor, "go— *believe* in Jesus Christ—and save your soul." (*The Wilmington Almanack . . . for . . . 1792* (23382))

A Jew and a Christian were conversing familiarly by the side of a well, when the former happened to fall in without receiving much hurt, and the Christian flew for a ladder to help him out. As he was eagerly endeavouring to put it down into the well, "It is not worth while," (says the Jew) "I will make no use of your ladder, today is Saturday." He remained therefore up to the chin in water till next morning when his friend came to know how he had fared during so cool a night. "The ladder! the ladder!" (cries the Jew) "for the love of God bring back the ladder!" "Heaven forbid!" replies the Christian) "today is Sunday." (*Beers's Almanac . . . for . . . 1794* (25152))

The celebrated Montesquieu, being one day at the house of a Jew, who was a rich banker, found him busily employed in sharpening a knife destined for performing some act of Jewish discipline. Montesquieu having asked him why he sharpened his knife with so much care, he replied, "because Moses had commanded that it should have no teeth." Montesquieu then bid him continue his operation: and when the scrupulous Jew was satisfied, the president took out a magnifying glass and shewed him abundance of large teeth where the naked eye could discover nothing but a fine edge. "Ah sir," cried the frightened Israelite, "it is a real saw; I am quite unhappy; I must begin my labor again." "Be easy," replied Montesquieu, "and consider your knife as properly sharpened; he who made your laws did not use spectacles." (*The Gentlemen's and Ladies' Diary, and Almanac . . . for . . . 1800* (35642))

A Jew, joking with a Christian, struck him on the cheek, and said, "Now turn the other as your gospel commands." But the Christian gave him a sound drubbing. The Jew cried, "This is not in the gospel."—"Aye," said the Christian, "but it is in the comment." " *Curse the comment,*" said the Jew, "it is harder than the text." (*The United States Almanac, for . . . 1800* (36599))

E. Others

No nation assumes so many Christian names as the Spaniards. A poor Don Quixote, who had no other company or attendant but the wretched jade upon which he was mounted, reached, with much difficulty, a small village in France, called Quivot, where there was but one little inn. As it was midnight when he arrived, he applied himself with great noise and diligence to the gate. The host, waking at last, looked out of the window and called, "Who's there?"

"Here is," answered the Spaniard, "Don Sancho, Alphonso, Ramiro, Juan, Pedro, Carlos, Francisco, Domingo de Roxas, de Stuniga, de las Fuentes."

The landlord, who knew he had but one empty bed, told him briskly he had not room for so much company; and so returned to his rest. In vain did the Spaniard bawl and argue. He was obliged to move two leagues further for an opportunity to rest. (*Father Abraham's Almanack, for . . . 1776* (14428))

The Chinese are so excessively addicted to gaming that they not only play very high; but when they have lost, scruple not to stake their wives and children, whom, if they lose, they resign to the winner, till they can advance as much money as they staked for: How many Englishmen would be glad to game away their wives and never reclaim them. (*Beers's Almanac . . for . . . 1794* (25152))

Whenever we see any thing ridiculous in the opinion or practice of foreigners we should turn out observations to ourselves, and enquire whether we have no absurdities to correct.—We laugh at the worshippers of Diane, *but what do we worship?* (*The Farmer's American Almanac for . . . 1798* (31786))

An unlettered son of Caledonia, at a public house in Palmertown, a short time since, where the conversation of the company turned on the politics of the day, gave the following sentiment, on being questioned as to his political tenets. Rising and taking up his glass—" *I denna ken about politics: Here's* FRIENDSHIP IN MARBLE—INJURY IN DUST." (*The United States Almanac, for . . . 1798* (32296))

A Scotchman, very fond of calves heads, cooked turtle fashion, was one day going home from market with a calf's head in his hand, which he held rather carelessly by the ear. Stopping to talk with a friend, a dog, watching his opportunity, [ste]pped up and snapping away the [head from the] hand of the honest Scot, fairly run off with it.—The owner, although *swift on foot,* soon found he was pursuing the dog to no purpose, and then bawled out, "Ah Tyke! ye may gang awa' wi'st; but mind boy, ye ha' na got the receipt for cooking calf's head!" (*The New Jersey and Pennsylvania Almanac, for...1798* (32833))

Ambrose Phillips observed, that painters always drew the same coloured skys whereas every country had its peculiar tints. "Aye," says a bystander, "Poland is the place for skies. There is Sobies sky, and Sarbien sky, and Jablon sky, and Podebra sky, and a thousand other skies." (*The Farmer's Calendar; or, Fry and Southwick's Almanack, for... 1798* (33172))

At the capture of the town of Oia, in the East Indies, by the Portugese in 1508, an officer of that nation, named Sylveria, observed one of the natives of a noble aspect, escaping by a private path, with a young woman of exquisite beauty. He ran instantly in order to secure them. The Indian did not appear at all apprehensive for his own safety; but after turning about to defend himself, he made a sign for his companion to fly. Her faithful love, however would not permit her to obey his injunctions. She resolutely refused to retire; assured her lover, that she would rather die on the spot or be a captive with him, than to make her escape alone. Sylveria, affected by the bravery of the one, and the magnanimity of the other gave them both liberty *to depart*; saying at the same time, to his officers and soldiers, "God forbid that my sword should destroy such noble and tender ties." (*An Almanack and Ephemeris, for...1799* (34155))

Mr. Alexander Wedderburn is one of those fortunate Scotchmen who has raised himself to high honours and rich emoluments; he left the Scottish bar as too barren a field, and, like many of his countrymen, transplanted himself to that more fruitful soil, London. With a considerable share of talents, and a very useful portion of confidence, he soon got into Parliament, became Attorney General, then a Lord Chief Justice, and is now Lord High Chancellor of England!

His Lordship prides himself on speaking the English language with more correctness than any of his countrymen, the late Lord Mansfield excepted.—One day, sitting on the bench, listening to a young Clerk who was reading the conveyances of an estate, and who, when he came to the word *enough*, pronounced it *enow*, his Lordship immediately interrupted him—"Hold, young man! you must *stand* corrected. En-o-u-g-h is, according to vernacular custom, called enuff; and, in like manner, so must *all* other English words be pronounced, which terminate in o-u-g-h; as for example, *rough, tough, &c.*"—The Clerk bowed, blushed, and went on for some time, when coming to the word *plough*, he, with a loud voice and a significant look at the bench, called it *pluff*! His Lordship saw his error, stroked his chin, and candidly said,—"Young Gentleman, I *sit* corrected." (*The Virginia and North Carolina Almanac, for...1800* (35239))

Chapter Five
Men, Women, Marriage and Sex

Several stories from early American almanacs deal with women and their relationships with men. It is clear that most of the stories were written by men, and that many of them express attitudes in comic form that few men would be unchivalrous enough to express straightforwardly. Several stories, for example, deal with the death of a wife, and many express the death as if it were a great benefit to the husband. A man who heard or told such a story would probably swear that he loves his own wife. Nevertheless he would laugh at the story and, possibly, expect his wife to laugh at it, too. Confronting a submerged attitude in humor, where it poses no threat, is often easier than confronting it straightforwardly.

If humor does serve such a purpose, then the citizens of America in the last quarter of the eighteenth century must have felt a great need to ventilate their feelings concerning what James Thurber would later call The War Between the Sexes. *In fact, there are more stories regarding the relationships between men and women than there are on any other topic. Including repetitions, more than four hundred comic items regarding such relationships appeared in the almanacs of that period. The overwhelming majority of such anecdotes express a misogynist attitude.*

The qualities attributed to women that were treated humorously include: shrewishness, talkativeness, curiosity, drunkenness, coquettry, infidelity and love of fashion. Relatively few stories dealt with womanly virtue, and those that did are, perhaps, even more indicative of the male attitudes that dominate the almanac stories. Only a very narrow kind of anecdote permits women to express themselves, presenting women as comic heroines, female wits, endowed with the same comic abilities that would be applauded in a man like Benjamin Franklin. Comic repartee, however is a trait associated not just with the Franklin's of the world; it is also associated with slaves and servants as an examination of some of the stories in earlier chapters will demonstrate. That women were allowed to shine in stories of witty repartee may only confirm their status in the male dominated humor of the almanacs.

Almanac humor, as it concerns the sexes, suggests that both men and women were expected to conform to certain roles. A woman should be modest, chaste and submissive. A man should be honest, dominant and attentive.

Women were often expected to fail in one or more aspects of their role.
If they did, the blame was sometimes placed on the husbands.

MEN, WOMEN, MARRIAGE AND SEX

A. The Value of Women

The wife of a farmer on an estate near Richmond was taken in labour: the farmer wished for a son, and waited in the next room for the intelligence: it proved a boy, and the man jumped from his chair, and clapped his hands with ecstasy. A few minutes after the maid servant came in, and said her mistress was delivered of another child, a fine girl; said the farmer with astonishment, "Well, well, we must endeavour to give it a bit of bread." A short while after the girl appeared again, and told him her mistress was delivered of a lovely boy! "What, another child!" said the farmer, almost frantic with surprize, "d—n it, Nanny, is your mistress pigging?" (*The Columbian Almanac, for...1797* (30244))

A farmer having settled in a country village on a little farm, gained the esteem of the whole neighbourhood. The first year was hardly expired when he lost a very fine cow, which was by much the best of all his cattle, and he was extremely mortified at it; but this was nothing to the grief he felt in a short time afterwards, when death also took away his wife. His neighbours thought they were obliged to comfort him; "Honest farmer," said one of them, "do not alarm yourself; the wife you lost was a good one, it is true, but there is as good to be had. I have three daughters for my part; take your choice of them." Another offered him a sister, another a niece.—"Lord have mercy upon us," replied the farmer, "it is better to loose one's wife than one's cow: My wife is hardly three hours dead, and here are half a dozen people already offering to supply her place for me; *but when my cow died, the devil a one spake of giving me another,*" (Beers' *Almanac for...1800* (35164))

B. Lovers

King Edgar, that great Monarch who is so famous in British story, fell in love as he made his progress through the kingdom, with a certain Duke's Daughter who lived near Winchester, and was the most celebrated beauty of the age. His Importunities and the Violence of his passion were so great, that the Mother of the young Lady promised him to bring her Daughter to his Bed the next Night, though in her heart she abhorred the infamous office. It was no sooner dark than she conveyed into his room a young Maid of no disagreeable figure, who was one of her Attendants,

and did not want to Address to improve the Opportunity, for the advancement
of her Fortune. She made so good use of her time, that when she offered
to rise a little before Day, the King could by no means think of parting
with her. So that finding herself under a necessity of discovering who she
was, she did it in so handsome a manner, that his Majesty was exceeding
gracious to her, and took her ever after under his protection: insomuch,
as our Chronicles tell us, he carried her along with him, and made her
his first Minister of State; and continued true to her alone, till his marriage
with the beauteous Elsinda. (*Hutchins Improved...for...1780* (16308))

A vigorous young officer, who made love to a widow, coming
a little unawares upon her once, caught her fast in his arms.
"Hey-dey," said she, "what? Do you fight after the French way,
take towns before you declare war?"
"No, faith, widow," (said he) "but I should be glad to imitate
them so far as to lie in the middle of the country, before you could resist
me." (*Bickerstaff's New-England Almanack, for...1780* (16672))

An amorous young man going by night into the city, and being
asked why he extinguished his torch at meeting with his mistress; "There
is no need of a torch when the sun shines." (*The Lady's Almanack, for... 1786*
(19748))

Epigram on a Lady's Girdle
That which her slender Waist confin'd,
Shall now my joyful Temples bind:
No Monarch but would give his Crown,
His Arms might do what *this* has done.
(*The Columbian Almanack, for...1788* (20225))

Epigram
He doted on Monimia's Charms,
He kiss'd her cheeks, her lips, her locket;
Then slumbering in the Fair-One's Arms,
She kist' the Fool, and pick'd his Pocket.
(*The Virginia Almanack, for...1791* (22315))

C. Vanity

A Lady's age happening to be questioned, she affirmed she was
but *forty*, and called upon a gentleman who was in company for his opinion.
"Cousin," said she, "don't you believe me when I say I am but forty?"
"I am sure, madam," replied he, "I ought not to dispute it; for I have

constantly heard you say so for above these ten years." (*Beers's Almanac...for...1796* (28250))

Such is the force of female curiosity, that Lady Wallace, who is never at a loss for an answer, one day affected to be wanting on that point; "Pray, Sir," said her ladyship to a country gentleman, "I am often asked what age I am, what answer should I make?" The gentleman immediately guessing her ladyship's meaning said, "Madam, when you are asked that question again, answer *that you are not yet come to years of discretion*." (*The New-England Almanac...for...1798* (32012))

An old lady beholding herself in a looking-glass, espying the wrinkles in her face, threw down the glass in a rage, saying, " *it was strange to see the difference of glasses; for*," says she, " *I have not looked into a true one these fifteen years.*" (*The Farmer's Almanack...for...1800* (36414))

D. Bundling

A Song upon Bundling. A reproof to those country young women who follow that reproachful practice, and to their Mothers that uphold them therein.

> Since bundling very much abounds,
> In many parts and country towns,
> No doubt, but some will spurn my song,
> And say I'd better hold my tongue.
>   But none I'm sure will take offence,
> Or deem my song impertinence,
> But only those who guilty be,
> And plainly here their pictures see.
>   Some maidens say, if thro' the nation,
> Bundling should go out of fashion,
> Courtship would lose its sweets; and they,
> Could have no fun till wedding day;
> It shan't be so, they rage and storm,
> And country girls in clusters swarm,
> And fly and buz like angry bees,
> And vow they'll bundle when they please.
>   Some mothers too will plead their cause,
> And give their daughters great applause,
> And tell them, tis no sin, nor shame,
> For we your mothers did the same:
> We hope the custome ne'er will alter,

But wish its enemies a halter.
        Dissatisfaction great appear'd
In several places where they've heard,
Their preachers bold, aloud declaim,
That bundling is a burning shame.
        This too was cause of direful rout,
And told, and talked of, all about,
That ministers should disapprove,
Sparks courting in a bed of love;
So justified the custom more,
Then e're was heard, or known before.
        The pulpit then it seems must yield,
And female valor take the field;
In places, where this custom long,
Increasing strength, has grown so strong,
When herein mothers bear a sway,
And daughters joyfully obey,
And young men highly pleased too,
Good Lord! What can't the devil do?
        Can this vile custom, ne'er be broke?
Is there no way to give a stroke?
To wound it or to strike it dead,
And girls with sparks not go to bed,
'Twill strike them more than preacher's tongue,
And let it be in common fame,
Held up to view, a noted shame.
        Young Miss if this your practice be,
I'll teach you now yourself to see;
You plead you're honest, modest too,
But such a plea will never do,
For how can modesty consist,
With shameful practice, such as this?
I'll give your answer to the life,
You don't undress like man and wife;
That is your plea we freely own,
But who your bondsman when alone?
That further rules you will not break?
And marriage liberties partake?
        Some really do, as I suppose,
Upon design, keep on some clothes,
And yet in truth I'm not afraid,
For to describe a bundling maid.
        She'll sometimes say, when she lies down,

She can't be cumbered with a gown,
And that the weather is so warm,
To take if off can be no harm;
The girl it seems had been at strift,
For widest bosom to her shift,
She gownless; when the bed they're in,
The spark nought feels but naked skin.
But she is modest, also chaste,
While only bare from neck to waist,
And he of boasted freedom sings,
Of all above the apron strings.
And where such freedoms great are shar'd
Are further freedoms feebly barred,
I leave for others to relate,
How long she'll keep her virgin state.
            Another pretty lass we'll scan,
That loves to bundle with a man,
For many different ways they take
Tho' modest rules they all will break,
Some clothes, I'll keep on, she will say,
For that has always been my way,
Nor would I be quite naked found,
With spark in bed for thousand pound.
But petticoats I've always said,
Were never made to wear in bed,
I'll take them off, keep on my gown,
And then I dare defy the town,
To charge me with immodesty,
While I so very cautious be.
            The spark was pleased with his maid,
Of apprehension, quick, he said,
Her witty scheme was keen he sware
Lying in gown, open before.
            Another maid when in the dark,
Going to bed with her dear spark,
She'll tell him that 'tis rather shocking,
To bundle in with shoes and stocking.
Not scrupling but she's quite discreet,
Lying with naked legs and feet,
With petticoat so thin and short,
That she is scarce the better for it.
But you will say, that I'm unfair,
That some who bundle take more care,

For some we may with truth suppose,
Bundle in bed with all their clothes.
       But bundler's clothes are no defence,
Unruly horses push the fence;
A certain fact I'll now relate,
That's true indeed without debate,
A bundling couple went to bed,
With all their clothes from foot to head,
That the defence might seem complete,
Each one was wrapped in a sheet;
But O! this bundling's such a witch,
The man of her did catch the itch,
And so provoked was the wretch,
That she of him a bastard catch't.
       Ye bundling lasses, don't you blush?
You hang your heads and bid me hush,
If you won't tell me how you feel,
I'll ask your sparks, they best can tell.
       But it is custom you will say,
And custom always bears the sway,
If I won't take my sparks to bed,
A laughing stock I shall be made.
       A vulgar custom'tis I own
Admir'd by many a slut and clown,
But'tis a method of proceeding,
As much abhord, by those of breeding.
(*Beers's Almanac for...1793* (24083))

E. Foolish Husbands

A blind man having contracted a violent passion for a certain female married her contrary to the advice of all his friends, who told him, that she was exceedingly ugly. A celebrated Physician, at length, undertook to restore him to sight. The Blind Man, however, despised his assistance. "I should be deprived of the love I bear to my wife; a love which renders me happy." "Man of God!" replied the Physician, "tell me which is of most consequence to a Rational Being, the attainment of *Happiness*, or the attainment of *Truth?*" (*An Astronomical Diary...for...1793* (24826))

A young parson lost his way in a forest, and it being very cold and rainy, he happened upon a poor cottage, and desired any lodging or hay to lay him in, and some fire to dry him. The man told him, he and his wife had but one bed, and if he pleased to be with them, he should be welcome. The parson thanked him, and kindly accepted it. In the morning, the [host] arose to go to market, and meeting with some of [his] neighbours, he fell a laughing. They asked him [what] made him so merry about the mouth? "Why," said he, "I can but think how ashamed the parson will [feel] when he awakes, to find himself left in bed with [his own] wife." (*Keatinge's Maryland Almanack for...1800* (35151))

F. The Battle of the Sexes

We men have many faults,
Poor women have but two;
There's nothing good they say;
There's nothing good they do.
(*The New-England Callendar: or Almanack, for...1793* (25026))

This world is a prison in every respect
Whose walls are the heavens in common;
The gaoler is sin, and the prisoners men,
And the fetters are nothing but—women.
(*The Columbian Almanac for...1796* (28784))

At an assize, where an indictment for an assault had been preferred against a woman for the ill usage of her husband, who was superanuated, his counsel, in the heat of declamation, happened to say that, "half the sex were devils!" But seeing a number of genteel females in the court after a very short pause, he went on—"But the other half are angels! and several of them are now present." (*The Town and Country Alamanac, (Revived...for...1800* (36443)))

G. Seduction

A young gentleman had got his neighbour's maid with child, the master, a grave man, came to expostulate with him about it. "Sir," says he, "I wonder you could do so;" " *Prithee, where is the wonder;*" says the other, " *If she had got me with child, you might have wondered indeed.*" (*Bickerstaff's Genuine Boston Almanack...* for...*1791* (23070))

A woman prosecuted a gentleman for a rape: upon trial the judge asked her if she made any resistance? "I cried out and please your lordship," said the woman. "Ay," said one of the witnesses, " *but that was nine months after.*" (*Bickerstaff's Genuine Boston Almanack...for...1791* (23070))

A girl who was a servant in a house reputed to be haunted, was suspected, and at last fairly convicted, of pregnancy; she fell on her knees before her mistress, craved forgiveness alleging indeed that she ought not to be blamed for it was entirely the ghostes's fault. "The ghost's fault!" exclaimed the mistress, "how could that possibly happen?" "Why indeed, Madam!" replied the simple girl, "the Ghost one night made a huge noise and almost scared me out of my seven senses. I told John how it *sarved* me, and he persuaded me how spirits never appeared, when two people slept together. So, as I liked his company better than the Ghosteses, and was mortally afraid of Ghosteses, I went along with him, and so, and so, indeed and indeed Madam, I should never have lost my *vartue*, if it had not been for fear of the Ghosteses." (*Beers's Almanac . . . for . . . 1794* (25152))

A young man was arraigned at the bar of a neighboring justice, for the growing evil of committing large depredations on a lady's chastity. Her honest father rated the damages in the premises at thirty pounds. The young man thought it was so common a thing that he ought to abate of the standard price and be content with fifty dollars.—But the Lady seeing her modesty insulted by this low valuation arose, and (Big with the Spirit of her cause) addressed the Judge in an elevated tone of voice, that she should insist on one hundred and twenty Dollars, as this was the very lowest price her Mother and all her sisters had always SET IT AT. (*The Kentucky Almanac, for . . . 1794* (25688))

An amorous young Fellow making very warm advances to a married woman. "Pray, Sir, be quiet," said she, "I have a husband that will not thank you for making him a cuckold." " *No, Madam,*" replied he, "*but I hope you will.*" (*The Columbian Almanac: or, The North American Calendar, for . . . 1798* (31956))

H. Early or Untimely Birth

A woman in twenty weeks after marriage, was brought to bed of a boy: "How now," says her husband, "methinks this is a little too soon." "No, husband," says she, "you mistake, for we married only a little too late." (*Bickerstaff's New-England Almanack, for . . . 1787* (20137))

A young countryman having a great opinion of the beauty and chastity of a neighbouring sheperdess, was induced to marry her; when a month after the celebration of the nuptials, she, to the surprise of her swain, was brought to bed of a fine boy. He immediately applied to a cradle-maker, and required that, as soon as convenient, he would make him a dozen cradles.—"good Heavens!" says the cradle-maker, "What will you do with them all?" "Do with them," says he, "I have been married but one month, and my wife has brought me a fine boy.—I am therefore determined to be prepared, for if she goes on at this rate, a shall want all the cradles in the course of the year." (*The Annual Visitor; Almanac, for... 1800* (35114))

A New Way of Reckoning

A sailor married a woman, staid with her the first night, went to sea the next day, and returned in three months, when he found her brought to bed of a boy. Jack stormed and called his wife a w——; but the nurse abused him in her turn for a sea booby that did not know how to reckon for a woman on shore, who counts by day and night. "Well," says Jack, "but that makes but six months, and she ought to go nine." "You fool," replies the matron, "You have forgot the three months you were at sea, only recollect that three months by day, and three at night, and three at sea, makes nine months, and you'll find your wife an honest woman." Jack could not follow this calculation, and was obliged to knock under, and allow it all to be right. (*The Citizen and Farmer's Almanac, for...1801* (37185))

I. Immodesty

Father Gardeau, a monk of St. Geneuief, and pastor of St. Stephen's on the hill, being rebuked at the little effects of his serious exhortations against the immodesty of women who uncovered their breasts in an excessive manner, began to accost them thus: "Cover yourselves, then, at least in our presence; for, in order that you should know it, we are flesh and blood like other men." (*Father Abraham's Almanack for... 1779*(16050))

J. Model Women

Harry the Fourth of France, asked a lady of his court, which was the way to her bedchamber. "Sir," said she, "the only way to my bedchamber is through the Church." (*Thomas's Massachusetts, Connecticut, Rhodeisland, Newhampshire & Vermont Almanack...for...1789* (21115))

A young gentleman, in one of the southern states, informed by a bill on the window of a house, that apartments were to be let knocked at the door, and attended by a pretty female, took a survey of the premises. "Pray, my dear," said the gentleman, smiling, "are you to be let with these lodgings?" "No, Sir," said she, "I am to be let alone." (*Carleton's Almanack...for...1794* (25261))

Timoclea, a Theban lady, being taken captive, and braving some ungenerous treatment from one of Alexander's Captains, shewed him a well, into which she said she had thrown her money and jewels; when he came near it, this courageous woman pushed him in headlong, and buried him under a heap of stones, which she threw upon him. Alexander, hearing of it, was so far from punishing her, that he immediately gave her her liberty. (*An Almanack, for...1798* (32941))

Pytheas, a daughter of Aristotle, being asked which is the most beautiful color, answered, "that of modesty." (*Keatinge's Maryland Almanack for...1800* (35151))

A young Gentleman and Lady, happening one Sunday to sit in the same pew.—During the course of the sermon the youth read something in the eyes of the fair, which made a much deeper impression on his soul, than the pious lecture of the parson: as love is seldom at a loss for an expedient, he presented her with the following verse in the second epistle of John: "And now I beseech thee, Lady, not as though I wrote a new commandment unto thee, but that which we had from the beginning, that we love one another." After perusal, she in answer, opened at the first chapter of Ruth, and 16th verse—"And Ruth said, entreat me not to leave thee, or to return from following after thee, for whither thou goest, I will go; and where thou lodgest, I will lodge; thy people shall be my people and thy God my God." Thus was the treaty proposed, which in a little time was fully ratified by the parson. (*Town and Country Almanac, (Revived)...for...1800* (36443))

K. Repartee by Women

A Sharp Sarcasm from a Young Lady to a Very Great Personage, at a Masquerade

A very great Personage, being at a masquerade, came up to a lady whose neck was bare: "Oh!" cries he, "let me put my hand on those pretty soft breasts."

"If you'll give me your hand," says she, "I will put it upon a softer place;" which he no sooner complied with than she put it on his own forehead and retired. (*Bickerstaff's Almanack, for...1779* (16166))

A gentleman happening to turn up against a house to make water, did not see two young Ladies, looking out of a window close by, till he heard them giggling. Then looking toward them, he asked, what made them so merry?

"Oh! Sir," said one of them, "a very *little thing* will make us laugh." (*Bickerstaff's New-England Almanack, for...1780* (16672))

A Mr. Wyman who was famed for nothing but his stupidity and indolence, as he was going from home one day, was desired by his wife, not to be gone so much—"She was afraid to be left alone." "Pough," said he, "Nought is never in danger." "I know that," said she, "but Nought's wife is." (*Wheeler's North American Calendar, or an Almanack, for...1791* (23073))

Once on a time I fair Dorinda kissed,
Whose nose was too distinguished to be miss'd,
My dear, says I, I fain would kiss you closer,
But tho' your lips say aye, Your nose says no Sir.
        The nymph was equally to fun inclin'd
And plac'd her lovely lilly hand behind,
Here, swain, says she, you may securely kiss,
Where is no nose to interrupt your bliss.
(*Hodge's North-Carolina Almanack, for...1793* (27793))

A son of a rich farmer, in the state of New Hampshire, who was possessed of a large share of diffidence paid his addresses to a young lady of his acquaintance, and after acquainting her with his intention, the lady conducted him to her department, and seating themselves at each end of the fire, the young hero, after a long silence, broke out in the following expression. "My father has the likelyest Bull Calf in town." The lady immediately made this reply. "I would have thanked him to have kept him at home." (*Town and Country Almanack, for...1795* (28067))

A person having purchased a watch, placed it in his fob, and strutting across the floor, says to his wife, "Where shall I drive a nail to hang my watch upon, that it may not be disturbed and broke?"—"I do not know a safer place," replied his wife, "than in our *meat barrel*, I'm sure no one will go there, to disturb it." (*Beers's Almanac...for...1797* (30044))

Lady C. Bruce, who is a *wit* in a certain way, on hearing of Lady Derby's pregnancy remarked, "that she always shewed a propensity to good breeding!" (*The Farmer's Almanack...for...1798,* (32921))

A clownish gentleman, who had courted a young lady, and agreed upon the marriage, espied a pretty mare grazing, which he would have into the bargain. The father being unwilling to part with the mare, the match was broke off. A twelve-month after, the wooer meets with the Lady at a fair, and would fain have renewed his old acquaintance; but she pretended ignorance at first, and said she did not know him. "No!" said he, "do you not know me? Why I was once suitor to you." "I ask your pardon, Sir," said she, "now I remember you: you came a wooing to my father's mare, and she is not married yet." (*Weatherwise's Almanack, for...1798* (33169))

Two gentlemen standing together, as a young lady passed by them, said one, "There goes the handsomest woman I ever saw." She hearing him turned back, and seeing him very ugly, said, "I wish I could in return, say as much of you." "So you may, madam," said he, *and lie as I do.*" (*Beers's Almanac for... 1799*(33388))

A Gentleman riding out one morning early in a place where he happened not to be acquainted; coming up by the side of a young woman who was carrying a pig in her arms, and hearing it scream violently, addressed her thus, " *Why my dear, your child cries amazingly.*" The young woman readily turning round and looking him in the face, said, with a smile upon her countenance, " *I know it, sir, it always does when it sees its daddy.*" (*The Town and Country Almanac, for... 1799*(34545))

Not long since, in London, as the Duchess of Gordon's happening to turn upon the consequences of a successful invasion by the French; several of the company mentioned the occupations they would adopt when all property should be seized by the Gallic freebooters. And many whimsical traders were started by the company, the Marquis of Huntley observed, that he would turn "garter maker for the ladies." "If that should be case," said the Duchess, "I fancy you would be *above* your business." (*The Gentlemen's and Ladies' Diary, and Almanac...for...1800* (35642))

L. Sexuality of Women

A young fellow, on the first night of his being married to a fine sprightly girl, when they were in bed, gave her a kiss, and asked her, "Well, my dear, shall we go to sleep, or how?"
"Oh my dear," replied the wife, "we'll How first, and go to sleep afterwards." (*Bickerstaff's New-England Almanack, for... 1778* (15706))

Miss S., one of the famous Miss H. "filles de joye," in dancing a masquerade at Carlisle-house, happened to trip and fall flat on her back;— Foote, who was in a domino, and near her, stooping to take her up, said "never mind it my pretty dear,—practice makes perfect." (*The Virginia Almanack, for... 1788*(20199))

A young gentleman playing at forfeits with some handsome young ladies, was commanded to take off a garter from one of them; but she, as soon as he had laid hold of her petticoats, ran away into the next room, where was a bed; "Now, Miss," said he, tripping up her heels, "I hear *squeaking.*" "*Bar the door, you fool,*" urged she. (*The Farmer's Almanack...for...1795* (27792))

A young couple were lately married in the state of New Jersey:— The groom being a votary of Bacchus, and overcome with liquor, forgetting to pay the customary fees to the officer that married them, retired and went to bed with his bride. He immediately fell asleep and so continued till some time in the morning, when the bride awoke and found him yet snoaring. She then arose and finding the groom's breeches, put them on under her cloaths, and withdrew from the room. Some short time after the groom awakened, and recollecting he had not paid the officer, looked about for his breeches, but could not discover them. He then called out aloud to his bride, who soon entered the room—" *My dear,*" (said he) *I cannot find my breeches!*"—She modestly replied, "*My dear Sir, you did not look in the right place!*"—And then drew up her cloaths, and shewed him where the breeches were. (*Beers's Almanac...for...1797* (30044))

A young woman being to take her oath before a justice of the peace, as a witness in some cause, the examiner asked her by what title he should set her down, whether maid, wife or widow? "O certainly a maid," said she, "for I never was married." He, seeing her a handsome, agreeable girl, asked her how old she was—she answered, "four and twenty." "How," said he, "four and twenty! have a care, my girl, what you say; remember you are now on your oath—may I safely set you down a maid at these years?" The girl, struck with the question, and considering a while with herself, said, "I pray you, sir; to avoid all mystakes, write me down a Young Woman." (*Franklin's Legacy: or, The New-York and Vermont Almanack, for...1799* (34376))

A country girl was sent to market to sell her butter, and being a pretty cherry cheeked fresh coloured girl, a gentleman took notice of her, bought all her butter, and insisted upon her drinking something with him, to which she with some reluctance, consented; and then he forced her to drink so much, that she was quite intoxicated;—he afterwards asked her to sleep with him that night, to which she very readily consented. The next morning when she returned home, her father and mother demanded the reason of her staying all night. She immediately told them the whole affair. "O you hussy," cryed they, "you are ruined!" "O mother," says the girl smiling, "I wish I was to be ruined so every night of my life, and live to the age of Methusala." (*The Farmer's Almanack, for...1799* (34968))

M. Male Sexuality (or lack of it)

The Bishop of Dorcetshire had a slovenly custom of keeping one hand always in his breeches, and being one day to bring a bill into the house of Peers, relating to a provision for officer's widows, he came with the papers in one hand, and the other, as usual, in his breeches; and beginning to speak, "I have something in my hand, my Lords," said he, "for the benefit of officer's widows."—Upon which the Duke of Wharton, immediately interrupting him, ask'd " *In which hand my Lord?*" (*Weatherwise's Town and Country Almanack, for...1787* (20126))

Nature whilst Jemmy's clay was blending,
Uncertain what the thing would end in,
Whether a female or a male,
A pin drop't in, and turn'd the scale.
(*Ames's Almanack, for...1792* (23121))

A country farmer, not long since having married a second wife, complained much of the rheumatism in his hips, He asked his wife one day, what was the matter with her goose, that she did not hatch; she answered shrewdly, that she supposed the gander had the rheumatism in his hips. (*The Farmer's Almanack...for...1796* (29626))

An humourist, observing the following inscription upon a wax-work shop, *Little children made here,* stepped in and asked the woman who kept the shop, if she wanted a *journeyman!* (*The New-York, Connecticut, and New Jersey Almanack...for...1799* (33390))

A mechanic, who kept a number of apprentices, whose wife was not possessed of the beauty of Helen, was very strict in meal time devotion; it happened, one day, at dinner time, the husband was absent: the lady looking round, and seeing no one at table to say grace, she thus addressed herself to the eldest apprentice; "John," says she, "since your master is absent, I believe you must supply his place." "I thank you madam," says John, "I had rather sleep with the boys." (*The Farmer's Almanack, for...1799* (34968))

King Charles the second, and the Duke of Ormrod, discoursing of the prettiest women in several countries, says the kind to the duke, "My Lord, you have pretty women in Ireland, but they have very large legs."

" O that's nothing, please you, my liege, we lay them aside." (*The Columbian Almanac: or, The North American Calendar, for . . . 1800* (35321))

N. Marriage in general

Honest Sim and his Wife, once to Sea took a Trip,
When a Sudden Cross Wind overset the light Ship,
Hand in Hand over Deck went this Couple together,
Susan sunk like a stone, Simon swam like a Feather;
"Thank my stars," says the man, safe escap'd from the flood,
" 'Tis a bad Wind, indeed, that blows no-body Good."
(*An Astronomical Diary, or Almanack for . . . 1789* (21455))

A gentleman in the country having the misfortune to have his wife hang herself on an apple-tree, a neighbour of his came to him and begged he would give him a scion of that tree—" *For, who knows,*" says he," *but it may bear the same fruit.*" (*Hutchins Improved: being an Almanack . . . for . . . 1794* (25646))

An honest clergyman in the country, was reproving a married couple for their frequent dissensions, which were very unbecoming, both in the eyes of God and man, seeing you are both *one*; " *Both one!*" cried the husband, " *Were you to come by our door sometimes when we quarrel, you would swear we were twenty.*" (*The Kentucky Almanac, for . . . 1796* (28927))

A new and terrible species of punishment is suggested, by a contemporary in the case of Shuttlewood the polygamist, namely, to confine him for life with his four wives! In the plentitude of benevolence, we recommend hanging or transportation. (*An Astronomical Diary or Almanac, for . . . 1797* (30921))

A Fidler and his wife, who had rubbed through life as most couples usually do, sometimes good friends, at others not quite so well, one day happened to have a dispute, which was conducted on both sides with becoming spirit. The wife was sure she was right, and the husband was resolved to have his own way. What was to be done in such a case?—The quarrel grew worse by explanations, and at last the fury of both rose to such a pitch, that they made a vow never to sleep together in the same bed for the future. This was the most rash vow that could be imagined; for they still were friends at bottom, and besides they had but one bed in the house; however resolved they were to go through with it, and at night the fiddle case was laid in bed between them, in order to make a separation.

In this manner they continued for three weeks; every night the fiddle case being placed as a barrier to divide them.

By this time, however, each heartily repented of their vow, their resentment was at an end, and their love began to return, they wished the fiddle case away, but both had too much spirit to begin. One night, however, as they were both lying awake with the detested fiddle case between them, the husband happened to sneeze, to which the wife, as is usual in such cases bid God bless him; "Aye, but," (returned the husband) "woman, do you say that from your heart?" "Indeed, I do my poor Nicholas," cried his wife. "I say it with all my heart." "If so then," (says the husband) "we had as good remove the fiddle case." (*The New-England Almanac- ...for...1798* (32012))

A gentleman asked a school master in Boston why he did not marry? "Why," says he, after pausing a few moments, "You take two dogs; and tie a large bone to the tail of one of them, and which do you think will go with the most ease?" (*The Town and Country Almanack, for...1798* (33168))

A young lady having buried an old husband who she married for money, ordered a carver to make a statue of wood, as much like him as possible, which, with much seeming regard for his memory, she every night placed by her side in bed. In the mean time, a young gentleman who was violently enamoured with our young widow, prevailed on the maid, by the help of a few guineas, to lay him in the place of Old SIMON: (as the beloved block was called). The widow went to bed, and after her usual manner cast her arms over her dear husband's statue, and finding it warm she crept still closer; till at last she was convinced that it was a better bed fellow than Old SIMON. In the morning the maid called as usual, to know what she would have for dinner. "Why, Susan," (says she) "I think you must dress the Turkey that was brought in yesterday, boil a leg of mutton and cauliflower, and get a handsome dish of fish." "Madam," (says the maid) "we have not wood enough to dress so much victuals." "Why, then," (replied the mistress) "you must e'en burn Old SIMON." (*The Farmer's Calendar; or, Fry and Southwick's Almanack, for...1798* (33172))

Two friends who had not seen each other for a long time met one day by accident—"How do you do?" says one—"So, so," (replies the other) "and yet I was married since you and I were together."—"That is good news."—"Not very good; for it was my lot to choose a termagant."—"It is a pity."—"I hardly think it so; for she brought me two thousand pounds."—"Well, there is comfort."—"Not much; for with her fortune I purchased a quantity of sheep, and they are all dead of the rot."—"That indeed is distressing."—"Not so distressing as you may imagine: for by the sale of their skins I got more than the sheep cost me." "In that case you are indemnified."—"By no means, for my house and all my money have been destroyed by fire."—"Alas! this is a dreadful misfortune."—"Faith, not so dreadful; for my wife and house were burned together." (*Franklin's Legacy: or, The New-York and Vermont Almanack, for. . .1799* (34376))

Mrs. K——, saying to her husband, that she was sure if she died, rather than live single, he would marry, though't were the devil's daughter. "No madam," said he, "I should not chuse to marry twice into the same family." (*An Astronomical Diary, Calendar, or Almanack, for. . .1799* (34616))

An old man hearing the bans of marriage published between one of his sons and a neighbor's daughter, on a Sunday while at meeting, as he was, until that time, a stranger to the connection, he was induced to say, as soon as they got home, "Well, Nathan, what's to pay now?" "There's nothing to pay father," said Nathan, " *but there's something coming.*" *(The Farmer's Almanac, for. . .1800* (35167))

Not long since, in Liverpool, a couple were going to be married, and had proceeded as far as the church yard gates, the gentleman stopped his fair comrade with the following unexpected address: "Mary, during our courtship I have told you *most* of my mind, but not *all* of my mind— when we are married, I shall insist on three things." "What are they?" asked the astonished lady—"In the first place, says he, "I shall lie alone; secondly, I shall eat alone; and lastly, I shall find fault when there is no occasion— can you submit to these conditions?" "Oh yes, Sir, very easily," she replies, "for if you lie alone, I *shall not*; if you eat alone, I shall *eat first*; and as to finding fault without occasion, that, I think, may be prevented, for I will take care that you shall never *want occasion.*" They were married, and the writer of this wishes them much happiness. *(Franklin's Legacy: or, The New-York and Vermont Almanack for. . .1800* (35169))

A short time since, a young fellow who paid his addresses to a lady, carried things so far, as not only to be asked at church, but to stop short in the marriage ceremony, by answering "No!" to the important question of, "Wilt thou have this woman to thy wedded wife?"—Outraged at this affront, the young lady thought of revenging the insult by silent contempt; but she had not long retired to her father's house, before the young gentlemen, who found the want of much pleasure and entertainment in the loss of her conversation, made several concessions and apologies, and regained the leave of visiting her as usual. Still he did not intend marriage, but though this was kept a secret from the lady in their first interview, she did not fail to reproach him handsomely with his conduct; and at the same time proposed that to make proper amends for the affront she had received, he should again approach the altar, and voluntarily give her the same opportunity of refusing him, as he had before made use of in rejecting her. This proposal was accepted; but, much to his surprize, her answer to "Wilt thou have this man to thy wedded husband?" was, " *I will*," instead of a negative; so that the gallant was married in spite of his own subtlety. (*The Philadelphia Almanac, for . . . 1800* (35728))

A countryman reading the Bible to his wife, where it is stated that Solomon had *three hundred wives and seven hundred concubines*, the good woman, in a tone of surprise, said she was sure he did not read it right, and insisted upon looking at the passage herself; when, having conn'd it over two or three times, and satisfied that it was so, she looked up in her husband's face, and chucking him gently under the chin, exclaimed, "Eh! What a simple Solomon wouldst thou make!" (*The Connecticut Pocket Almanac, for . . .1800* (36384))

Conjugal Love

An Affectionate Wife—An honest schoolmaster near London, having a wife whom he loved very affectionately, was so fortunate as to perceive that she conceived a tendre for a smart young fellow whom he engaged as usher. The poor man was rendered so miserable by the perfidy and ingratitude of his rival that he determined to destroy himself. This resolution, after some prefatory reproaches, he communicated to his wife, declaring that he would tuck himself up with his neckcloth. To this the effected lady replied, "Alas! my dear, consider that neckcloth is very old, and can never sustain your weight. Do stop a moment, my love, till I reach you your new cravat!"

A Tender Husband—A gentleman in the city was for some time yoked to a rante who had that unable quality of never receiving or supposing herself to receive any injury without breaking silence. One day observing her consort whispering something to the maid, She instantly fixed her fangs in his face, tore up his hair by the roots, and in short suffered passion so much to get the better of her, that she was actually suffocated by its violence. The penitent poor husband was, no doubt, so overcome with grief at the sad accident, that he forgot to use any of those methods recommended by the Humane Society for the recovery of persons in his wife's situation. Indeed, so anxious was he for her everlasting repose that he gave instant instructions for her funeral, directing most particularly that she should be buried with her face downward! Being asked the reason of this, "Why," replied he, "if she should happen to awake, the more she scratches, the deeper she goes!" (*The American Almanac, for... 1801* (36808))

O. Women as talkers

A fellow hearing one say, according to the Italian Proverb, that three women made a Market with their chatting:
"Nay then," said he, "add my wife to them, and they will make a Fair." (*Hutchin's Improved...for...1776* (14125))

A woman's charms may fade away,
Her eyes grow dim, her teeth decay;
But, while she breathes the vital gale,
'tis strange her *tongue* should never fail.
(*Dunham and True's Almanac for...1796* (28602))

A gentleman sat down to write a deed, and began with. " *Know one woman by these presents.*"—"You are wrong." says a bystander, "it ought to be, 'Know all men.' " "Very well," answered the other, "if one woman knows it all men will of course." (*Beers's Almanac... for...1797* (30044))

Epitaph
Beneath this stone, a lump of clay,
        Lies Arabella Young,
Who on the twenty fourth of May
        Began to hold her tongue.
(*Dunham and True's.. Almanac, for...1797* (32065))

Milton was asked by a friend, whether he would instruct his daughters in the different languages to which he replied, "No, Sir, one tongue is sufficient for a woman." (*Father Abraham's Almanac, for.. 1799* (34630))

There is something irresistably pleasing in the conversation of a fine woman; even though her tongue be silent the eloquence of her eyes teaches wisdom. The mind sympathizes with external grace, vibrates into respondent harmony. (*The United States Almanac, for...1800* (36599))

P. Shrewishness

Epitaph
Beneath this rugged stone doth lie,
The rankest scold that e'er did die;

Whose softest word to dearest friend,
Would make his hair stand bolt on end!
You'd think storms rising when she sung;
Thunder was music to her tongue!
When real storms in her did rise,
Lighting was twilight to her eyes!
Her mildest look so fierce a sight
Great chance you'd catch an ague by't
And when her person mov'd—huge rock!
No earthquake gave so fierce a shock!
Where she abides, seek not to know;
If they want sulphur she's *below*;
If she's above—Gods hear my prayer,
And send me anywhere but *there*.
(*The Federal Almanac, for...1793* (24418))

An old countryman, named Dobin, who was married to a termagant wife, went one Sunday to the parish-church, and heard the parson preach from the following words, "Take up your cross and follow me." Dobin was more than ordinary attentive to the discourse, and as soon as church was done, went directly home, and taking his wife upon his back by force, ran as fast as he was able after the parson; who seeing how the fellow was loaded, and following him, asked him, "What was the reason of his carrying his wife in that manner?" "Why, what a plague," cries Dobin, "has your memory forgot already? did not your reverence tell us, that we must take up our cross and follow me? and I am sure this is the greatest cross I have in the world, so pray Mr. Parson keep your word, or I'll follow you to the devil." (*The Pennsylvania, New-Jersey, Delaware, Maryland and Virginia Almanac...for...1799* (34631))

A clergyman, who in the matrimonial lottery had drawn much worse than a *blank*, and, without the patience of Socrates, had to encounter the turbulent spirit of Xantippe, was interrupted in the middle of a *curtain-lecture*, by the arrival of a pair, requesting his assistance to introduce them to the *blessed* state of wedlock. The poor priest, actuated at the moment by his own feelings and particular *experience*, rather than a sense of cannonical duty, opened the book, and began. " *Man, that is born of woman, hath but a short time to live, and is full of trouble, &c. &c.*" repeating the *burial* service. The astonished bridegroom exclaimed, "Sir! Sir! you mistake, I came here to be *married*, not *buried!*" "Well," (replied the clergyman) "if you insist upon it, I am *obliged* to marry you—but, believe me, my friend, you had *better* be *buried*." (*Stoddard's Diary or, the Columbia Almanack, for...1800* (35173))

Q. Coquettry

At a late Ball given in the vicinity of Richmond, Miss S——, a finished coquette, asked a gentleman near her, whilst she adjusted her tucker, "Whether he could *flirt* her FAN," which he held in his hand? "No, Madam," answered he, and he proceeded to use the machine immediately, "but I can *fan* a FLIRT." (*Father Tammany's Almanac for...1793* (25059))

A gentleman asked a lady who made a very large acquaintance among the beaux and pretty fellows, what she could do with them all? "Oh," said she, "they pass off like the waters:" " *And, pray, madam,*" replied the gentleman, *"do they all pass the same way?"* (*The Farmer's Almanack...for...1795* (27792))

A wanton Gentlewoman reproached her Brother with his Passion for gaming, which she said, was the Ruin of him: "When will you leave off gaming?" says she to him: "When you leave off coquetting." "Oh? unhappy Man," replies the Sister; "then you are likely to game all your life-time." (*Hutchins Improved: being an Almanack...for...1800* (35649))

R. Infidelity

A young fellow, after having an affair with a girl, said, "How shall we do, Bess, if you should prove with child?"
"Oh, very well," said she, "for I am to be married tomorrow." (*Bickerstaff's New-England Almanack, for...1778* (15706))

A peasant whose wife was in labor, approached her bed and endeavored to console her; the wife, in the height of her pains, seeing him cry: "Ah! my friend," said she to him, "do not grieve so much to see me suffer, for I know very well you are not the cause of it." (*Father's Abraham's Almanack for...1779* (16050))

A married lady was seized with a singular longing for charcoal, and absolutely eat several pieces. In about four months afterwards, she was delivered of a fine mulatto boy, and the fond husband imputed the dusky hue to charcoal. Her Ladyship's footman is a stout African. (*The Columbian Almanack...for...1791* (22912))

Said buxom Joan, to husband Dick,
"If man and wife one creature be
"To cuckold you's a loving trick,

"Since you the pleasure share with me!"
"You're right," said Dick, and twig of tree,
About her sides with vigor flew,
"Since you the the pleasure share with me,
"I'll kindly share the pain with you."
(*Beers's Almanack...for...1792* (23163))

A gentleman seeing his footman with an old greasy hat, slouching over his shoulders, "Sirrah," says he, "who gave you that cuckold's hat?" "Indeed, sir," says John, "it was my mistress gave it me, and told me it was one of yours." (*The Farmer's Almanack...for...1796* (29626))

A True Story

The wife of a young deacon in the town of Swanzy in the State of New-Hampshire, and a young widow being one evening at the house of a sick woman in the neighbourhood, it was agreed that the Deacon's wife should tarry all night, to take care of the patient. The widow, on returning home, had to pass the house of the Deacon, when the idea suggested itself, that it was a convenient opportunity to be better acquainted with the good man. Perhaps she might recollect the words of Rachel to the patriarch Jacob, "give me children or else I die." However this might be, she went into the house and got into bed with the good man as his wife. As she rose in the morning before it was very light, she was asked the reason of her early rising? She replied, that she had lost her bonnet, and must go and seek it before any person travelled the road: and so went out. Soon after the Deacon's wife came in. "Have you found your bonnet," said the husband? "What bonnet" rejoined the wife? "Why," said he, "did you not tell me that you had lost your bonnet?" "No." This dialogue led to an unravelling of the plot; and it was mutually agreed to say nothing of the affair. A while after, it was discoverable that the widow had been playing the wanton; and she was obliged to confess the fact, with all the circumstances. But as the Deacon appeared to have been imposed upon, by the artifice of the woman, the church to which it belonged, in the spirit of Christianity, overlooked the affair. The child was taken home by the honest Deacon, and by him maintained and brought up. (*Beers's Almanac...for...1797*(30044))

An Alderman of the city of Dublin, having some little doubt about the chastity of his wife and whether he was the father of the child, of which she was pregnant, exacted an oath from her, that she had never carnally known any person, except himself, since she was rocked in the cradle, to the present hour; alledging, that if she refused to take such an oath, he should think his suspicions were well grounded, and would never cohabit with her more. The lady was shocked at such an unreasonable request from the dear partner of her bed: and after expressing her astonishment that he should entertain the least suspicion of her honour, confided with her nurse, how to qualify an oath so as to avoid downright perjury, and yet be sufficient to remove her husband's doubts. The nurse like an able councellor, recommended the following expedient:—"Get into the cradle," said she, "which stands in the next room, and I'll rock you for a space of one or two minutes; you may then without any scruple of conscience, take the oath that your foolish husband prescribed." The lady generously rewarded the nurse for her ingenious device; and told her spouse, that she should gladly make the affidavit he proposed, if it would in the least contribute to his happiness—she did so, and they have ever since lived upon very happy terms together. (*The Annual Visitor; or Almanac, for . . . 1800* (35114))

A bridegroom, the first night he was in bed with his bride, said, "When I solicited your chastity, if you had granted, I would not have married you."—"Faith, I thought as much," (said the cunning lady), "but as I had been cheated two or three times before, I was determined not to be fool'd again!" (*The Virginia and North Carolina Almanack for . . . 1801* (37046))

S. Fashion and Dress

A lady, distinguished for the figure she made in the fashionable world, was thrown in the utmost agitation of mind upon a Caterpillar's falling from a branch of a tree upon her bosom: "Away, frightful detested thing," she cried, "my nature shudders at thee; it is thy horrid race that destroys the hopes of the husbandman by consuming the gaubage, Hence, vile insect, hence." The Caterpillar apologized with great humility for the accident—"As to my ugly appearance," said he, "Your Ladyship may be assured it will not continue long; I shall soon be changed into a butterfly, and range the ambient air, adorned with a variety of beautiful tints, which will, no doubt, make me very very amiable in the eyes of such fine Ladies as yourself, who, it is said, exactly resemble our tribe in their transformation; that is to say, you are too often Caterpillars coming out of your beds, and butterflies after you rise from your toilets." (*The Pennsylvania, Delaware, Maryland, and Virginia Almanack . . . for . . . 1788* (20898))

Epigram on a Lady Writing Verses with a Hole in her Stocking"

> To see a lady of such grace,
> With so much sense and such a face,
> So slatternly is shocking;
> O! if you would with Venus vie,
> Your pen and poetry lay by,

And learn to mend your stocking.
(*Father Hutchins Revived, for...1793* (24416))

Epigrams on the Ladies Pads:
When women's minds were undefiled and chaste,
Even wives would blush to shew a *swelling waist.*
But now the PADS, that give the *fashion'd swell,*
Mere Misses *wants* and *wanton wishes* tell.
Tho' great in size, their modesty is small,
They *rise* to shew, how easily they *fell.*

Says *Laura* to *Kitty,* while fixing her PAD,
"A *natural one* must be charming Egad."
"Yes," laughing, said Kitty, "for who can neglect,
To advert to the *cause,* when they see the *effect.*"
(*The Virginia Almanack, for...1794* (25112))

Mrs. W——, walking on one of the wharves at New York, jocosely asked a sailor, why a ship was always called she? "On faith," says the son of Neptune, "because the *rigging* costs much more than the *hull.*" (*Isaiah Thomas's Massachusetts, Connecticut, Rhodeisland, Newhampshire & Vermont Almanack...for...1799* (34652))

T. Margaret Yeh Evan

The Hardy Welsh Sports Woman

Margaret Yeh Evan, of Penllyn, who inhabited a cottage on the borders of Llanberris Lake, was the greatest hunter, shooter, and fisher, of her time; she kept at least a dozen of terriers, grey hounds and spaniels, all excellent of their kinds; she killed more foxes in one year than all of the confederated hunts do in ten; rowed stoutly, and was queen of the lake; played excellently on the violin and knew all our old music; nor did she neglect the mechanic arts; for she was a very good joiner; and notwithstanding she was seventy years of age, was the best wrestler in the neighborhood, and few young men dared to try a fall with her. (*The Annual Visitor, or Almanac, for...1801* (36842))

Chapter Six
Stereotypes of Professionals

Physicians, clergymen, lawyers and politicians represent different kinds of authority. Comic stereotyping deflates their authority and shows that they are mere human beings with weaknesses and vices like the rest of us, but with stereotyped ways of expressing their weaknesses and vices.

A clergyman, for example, may be as frightened of death as anyone else, even though his profession requires him to teach the joys of life after death. Physicians make mistakes, but they bury them. Lawyers may also be liars, an easy pun, and one that some writers of stories for the almanacs believed expressed a truth. Politicians had to court the favor of the masses in order to be elected. Like lawyers, they were often considered to be dishonest.

Comic stories about the clergy make use of many of the same comic traits that are seen in such stories today. The almanac stories present some clergy as long winded and boring, others as hypocritical, overly prideful, lacking in constancy of faith or simply susceptible to foolish mistakes. A few stories appear anti-Catholic, but most are neutral toward any specific religion. Witty repartee appears in some stories, either uttered by the clergyman or in response to him. A small number of stories represent good clergymen. A few stories concentrate on the children of clergymen. Such children, it appears, are often wild and unruly. In this chapter, deacons and others who are not strictly clergy are included because they share many clerical characteristics.

Like the clergyman, the lawyer and his associates have long been known as stock figures in British humor. In the eighteenth century both Henry Fielding and Tobias Smollett, among others, made use of the British tradition of stereotyped comic lawyers.

American almanac humor of the late eighteenth century also makes use of the lawyer and other court officials as stock comic characters. Only the clergyman appears in more stories than does the lawyer or justice, and the lawyer or justice is more often the butt of the humor than is the sometimes model clergyman.

Although a very few stories present lawyers who have the virtues of ingenuity and love of the law, the overwhelming majority of stories about lawyers and justices attack them for such evils as browbeating witnesses,

*impertinence, cupidity, lying, using jargon and, sometimes, even for being
aligned with the devil.*

*Physicians have also appeared as stock comic characters in English and
Continental humor for hundreds of years. The nature of the physician's
profession may provide part of the reason for his popularity as a comic
figure. At best, the physician's battle is a losing one. All men die sooner
or later, and physicians cannot alter that fact. Given the state of medical
science in the eighteenth century, however, people were more likely to die
sooner than later; the futility of the physician's cause became one of his
comic traits.*

*While several comic items deal with the inability of the physician to
prevent death, others showed physicians who did not even try or who actually
hurried death along. Some were so inflexible as to prescribe the same medicine
for every illness.*

*Politicians were still relatively new in the eighteenth century, but
stereotypes were already being worked out for them. Since they were associated
with the law, they shared some of the characteristics of lawyers. Since they
had to make speeches, they could be as long winded and as boring as a
clergyman. Since they had to be elected, they had to please the voters and
those who could deliver votes. Very few were portrayed as strictly honest.*

CLERGYMEN
A. Hypocrisy of clergymen

A monk, being out of patience at fasting too long, bethought himself
of roasting an egg by the heat of a lamp. The abbot, who was making
his visits, saw through the keyhole, the monk at his little cookery, entered
abruptly and reprimanded him severely, where the monk excused himself,
saying that it was the devil who had tempted him; and had inspired him
with the invention. The devil immediately appears in person, who was hid
under the table, saying "You are a liar, you dog of a monk, this trick is
not my invention, it is you who taught me it." (*Father Abraham's Almanack
for...1779* (16050))

In every country and order of men, there are some unworthy persons:
One such—a clergyman in Scotland, cast his eye on a couple of acres of
land, on which a poor widow woman lived. He went and took it over her
head, by offering a larger rent. Soon after, at a catechizing in the kirk, he
asked her, "How many commandments are there."—"Nine, Sir."—"Nine!
I thought there had been ten, Janet"—"Yes, sir, there were ten; but you
took away the tenth, when you took my twa acres o'er my head." (*Father
Tammany's Almanac, for...1787* (20160))

A certain vicar, while he preach'd
    Of patient Job did speak;
When he came home he found, sad chance!
    His cask had sprung a leak.

Enrag'd—his wife did him advise
    · Job for a pattern choose;
But he reply'd—"Job ne'er had such
    A tub of ale to lose."
(*Thomas's Massachusetts, Connecticut, Rhode-Island, New-hampshire and Vermont Almanack...for...1791* (22537))

    A merchant in New-York, enquired of a countryman the character of a Deacon, his neighbor, who made a great profession of religion, and had applied to the merchant for a credit. The countryman replied, that *Godward*, the Deacon was accounted a very honest upright man; but *Manward*, he was a little *twistical* or so. An excellent description of thousands of our neighbors. (*Beers's Almanac...for...1794* (25152))

    In a storm at sea, Mr. Swain, chaplain of the Rutland asked one of the crew, if he thought there was any danger? "O yes," replied the sailor, "if it blows as hard as it does now, we shall all be in heaven before twelve o'clock tonight." The chaplain, terrified by the expression, cried out, "O God forbid." (*The New-Hampshire and Massachusetts Pocket Almanack, for...1794* (25933))

    A certain Reverend Refugee Doctor, while at New York, had the care of the souls of one or more men of war, of one or more regiments, and of a church at the same time. This said Doctor, to ease his conscience, *once* went on board one of the men of war, to give them prayers and a sermon and took for his text these words, "My yoke is easy and my burden is light." A Jack Tar who was present, broke out, "Yes, I think the burthen is d—d light, to make us pay you for praying and preaching the whole year, and you give us but one service for our money." (*An Almanack for...1794* (26229))

    The celebrated Whitfield once told a congregation, that he himself should bear witness against them at the tribunal of heaven. "Aye," says a sailor, "Just like the old Bailey for all the world— *The greatest rogue turns king's evidence.*" (*The Farmer's Calendar; or, Fry and Southwick's Almanack, for...1798* (33172))

A country curate, who had much insisted in an afternoon sermon, that reason was given to man for a bridle, to curb and restrain his passion, happening the same evening to take so large a dose at a christening that he was obliged to be carried home; the next morning one of his parishioners asked him, what he had done with his *bridle* over night, he replied, " *I just took it off to drink.*" (*Beers's Almanac for . . . 1799* (33388))

A certain priest in a rich abbey in Florence, being a fisherman's son, caused a net to be spread every day on a table to his apartment, to put him in mind of his origin: the abbot dying, this dissembled humility procured him to be chosen abbot, after which the net was used no more. Being asked the reason, he answered, "there is no occasion for the *net now* the *fish* is *caught.*" (*The Kentucky Almanac, for . . 1799* (33954))

A parson standing in need of a new wig, his old one defying all farther assistance of art; he went over to Canterbury, and applied to a barber, young in business to make him one. The tradesman who was just going to dinner, begged the honour of his new customer's company to his meal: to which the parson very readily consented. After dinner a large bowl of punch was produced, and the reverence guest, with equal readiness, joined in its demolition: when it was out, the barber was proceeding to business, and began to handle his measure—when the parson desired him to desist, saying he should not make his wig. "Why not," exclaimed the astonished shaver, "Have I done any thing to offend you, Sir?" "Not in the least," replied the parson: "but I find you a very honest, good natured fellow: so I will take some body else in—had you made it, you never would have been paid." (*The Annual Visitor; or Almanac, for . . . 1800* (35114))

The Vicar of Bray, in Berkshire, being a catholic under the reign of Henry VIII, and a protestant under Edward VI, a catholic again under Queen Mary, and a protestant in the reign of Queen Elizabeth, was reproached as the scandal of his gown, by turning from one religion to another; "I cannot help that," replied the Vicar, "but if I have changed my religion, I am sure I have kept true to my principle, which is, to live and die the Vicar of Bray." (*An Astronomical Diary, Calendar, or Almanack for . . . 1801* (38550))

B. Boring Sermons

The famous Rabelais was in his last sickness when a reverend Prelate came to see him, and after tiring the languishing wit with a heap of stuff, he asked him, what was his chief complaint? "Want of sleep, my Lord," answered Rabelais. "And can you get no dormitives to do you good?" cried the Bishop. "Why, truly," says Rabelais, "I have tried a great many to no purpose; but I fancy if your Lordship would lend me a sermon which I heard you preach at the church of Notredame about three months ago, it would have the desired effect." (*Bickerstaff's Almanack, for . . . 1779* (16166))

A certain delirious man went to meeting one Sunday, and peacably seated himself in the gallery.—In sermon time, looking round the meeting house, observing some of the congregation sleeping, and having accidentally armed with a pocket full of rotten apples, he drew them forth one by one, taking aim, let them drive, flip in the faces of the sleeping Christians— This was repeated several times to the no small diversion of the audience— but the parson observing the movement above, "desired the people to take care of that crazy person," who pertly replyed, "You mind your preaching. I'll keep the dogs awake." (*The Columbian Almanac: or, The North-American Calendar, for . . . 1795* (26786))

Mr.——was not remarkable for his punctual attendance at worship. A friend once asked him why he was so frequently culpable in that respect? His reply, we think, was a little singular.—He said that *neighbour such a one, who sat near his pew, snored so intolerably that he could not sleep.* (*The Farmer's Almanack . . . for . . . 1795* (27792))

A clergyman who had often been retorted upon by his hearers for the tedious length of his sermons, one day, when he had a charity sermon to preach, chose the following for his text, "He that giveth to the poor, endeth to the Lord." The whole of his sermon was, " *If you like the security do it with your money.*" (*Beers's Almanac . . . for . . . 1797* (30044))

A minister in Massachusetts observing that the old people in the seats below were asleep, and the boys in the gallery were whispering and playing, he looked sternly at the young rogues, and with a stamp cried out, "Boys, be still there—you make such a racket, that the old men can't sleep." (*Webster's Calendar; or, The Albany Almanack, for . . . 1797* (31617))

A clerical gentleman remarkable for preaching many Sundays from one text, had nearly run through the year from these words, " *Peter's wife's mother lay sick of a fever.*" The church bell tolled early one morning. Mr. Minister dispatched a servant to enquire who was dead—The sexton pretended ignorance, but returned for answer, "That he believed it was *Peter's wife's mother*, as she had been sick for a long time." (*Stoddard's Diary: or, the Columbia Almanack, for . . . 1798* (31788))

Some time ago, at a yearly commencement in one of our Eastern States, the auditors were entertained part of the forenoon with a Hebrew oration. Being quite weary of the discourse, a parson addressed his companion, who happened to be a New England sea captain, that he wished the young man instead of facing the audience would address himself only to those that understood Hebrew,—"Do you so," said the tar, "then, by——Brother Jonathan, there would not be a single point of compass that would take him." (*Poor Richard Revived, or the Albany Almanack: for...1801* (38296))

C. Prideful clergymen

A young clergyman whose garb did not designate who he was, yet being very anxious to be known requested the company to guess at his occupation—they happened all to guess wrong—vexed at their stupidity, he exclaimed, "I'm the voice of one crying in the wilderness!" "I thought," said an arch wag, "that you resembled an owl." (*Poor Richard Revived: being the Farmer's Diary...for...1797* (31099))

A poor malefactor, in Newgate, was lately surprised, as he was searching the Bible very attentively, by his visitor, a Fanatic preacher: he said he was looking for a passage he could not find. "Give it me," said the pastor: "I can find any passage." "Can you so?" says the criminal: "why then I wish you would find me a PASSAGE OUT OF THIS CURST PRISON." (*The American Almanac, for... 1798* (31836))

A New-light preacher has generally a horrible whining tone in delivery. One of them, in his sermon, some time since, observed that a certain old lady appeared to be greatly affected by his preaching. After the exercises were over, he enquired what it was in his sermon that had so overcome her; and hoped his discourse had been instrumental in convicting and converting her sinful soul. "Why la!" replied the good old lady, "you make a noise so much like my husband's old cow, that died last week, that used to give always a pailfull of milk, that I could not help mourning for her." (*Franklin's Legacy; or, The Lansingburgh Almanack, for... 1798* (32690))

A young priest of greater pertness than wit, being asked in company how he came to take it into his head to enter the ministry? Said he, "The Lord had need of me," "that may be," replied a gentleman present, "for I have read that the Lord once had need of an *Ass.*" (*The New-York, Connecticut and New Jersey Almanack...for...1799* (33390))

In a select company, some little time since, the topic of conversation chanced to be what university each of the company was educated at: One was at Newhaven, another at Cambridge. "For my part," says a young clergyman, "I was educated at both universities:—Newhaven and Cambridge." "That puts me in mind," says an old doctor of divinity, "of a story I once heard, of a calf that sucked two cows." "And what was the consequence, pray?" says the young clergyman. "Why the consequence was," replied the doctor of divinity, "that he was a very great calf." (*Isaiah Thomas's Massachusetts, Connecticut, Rhodeisland, Newhampshire and Vermont Almanack...for...1799* (34652))

D. Foolish Statements by Clergymen

An old parson was reprimanding the gallants of the times, saying, "Beloved, the apparel which men now wear, makes them look like apes in their short breeches; and the ladies, forsooth, must have their gowns dangling half a yard on the ground, a very unseemly sight: Now, to rectify this disorder, you women should take up your coats; and you men should let down your breeches." (*The Columbian Almanac or, The North-American Calendar, for...1798* (31956))

A Scotch parson, in his prayer said, "Laird bless the great council the Parliament, and grant that they may hang together." A country fellow standing by, replied, "Yes, yes, with all my heart, and the sooner the better; and I am sure it is the prayer of all good people." "But, friends," said Sawney, "I don't mean as that fellow means, but pray they may hang together in accord and concord." "No matter what cord," replied the other, "so 'tis a strong cord." (*The United States Almanac, for...1799* (34546))

A chaplain to a Governor of Bengal, more remarkable for the goodness of his heart than the brilliancy of his wit, being, one day at the table of his patron, asked for a toast, with much simplicity, exclaimed "Alas; and a lack a day! What can I give?" "Nothing better," replied the Governor. "Come gentlemen, a bumper to the parson's toast—A *lass* and a *lack* a day." A lack of rupees is 100,000 pounds. (*The Annual Visitor; or Almanac, for...1800* (35114))

A clergyman took for his text these words, "the flesh, the world, and the devil," and began his sermon in the following manner; "I shall soft touch upon the flesh, pass lightly over the world, and hasten as fast as I can to the devil." (*The Farmer's Almanac, for...1800* (35167))

E. Wit of Clergymen

A certain Earl, more celebrated for his jollity than his religion, notwithstanding his chaplain was available, introduced a baboon, dressed up in the garb of a clergyman, in order to say grace; which conduct was very properly resented by the chaplain, who told his lordship, that he did not know till then that he had so near a relation in orders. (*The Pennsylvania Almanack, for.. 1788* (20751))

A country parson who had a great desire to disengage himself from a company of hungry gentlemen that came to his house, after he had told them, at first, that they were very welcome, and made a show of sending his servants, some of them to draw ale, and others to kill fowls, at the same time he took his surplice, and his prayer-book in his hand, and prepared himself to go abroad. "Where are you going Mr. Parson?" said the gentlemen. He answered, "I'll return in a minute, for I must go, whilst the dinner is making ready, to pray by a poor man, dying of the plague." And upon saying this, went out immediately. Upon which those spungers were so frightened, that they ran away immediately, full drive, and fled *as if the Plague had been at their heels. (Weatherwise's Almanack, for...1789* (21579))

As two clergymen were riding over Boston neck, when they approached the gallows, one pointing to it, said to the other; "What would be your unhappy situation, should Justice now take place?"—"Indeed, Sir," said the other, "I should be obliged to ride to Boston alone." (*Beers's Almanac...for...1794* (25152))

A venerable clergyman in a neighbouring state, grieved to see the doctrine of universal salvation prevailing in his parish, was desirous of preventing its progress by convincing Mr. M—, the preacher of the doctrine, that his system was unscriptural, and dangerous to society. For this purpose he requested the company of Mr. M— one evening, and being too old to manage the argument with dexterity himself, he desired a young clergyman of his acquaintance to attend and assist him.—The aged gentlemen opened the conversation of the evening by informing his younger brother in the ministry, that he has requested the company of Mr. M— and himself, in order to have the doctrine of universal salvation fairly discussed in his presence, for he thought Mr. M— might be convinced of his error, but he was too old to manage the debate—he therefore desired the young clergyman to enter upon the argument with Mr. M—. "Why, Sir," replied the gentleman with his usual address, "Jesus Christ says, 'he that believeth shall be saved, and he that believeth not, shall be damned;' the dispute, therefore, is wholly between Jesus Christ and Mr. M—, and I wish to be excused from an interference." (*The Farmers' Almanack, for...1798* (32114))

Lord Strangford, who stammered so much, was telling a bishop that sat at his table, that Balaam's ass spoke, because he was pri—est—"priest-rid, sir!" said a valet-de-chamber, who stood behind the chair, "my lord would say." "No, friend," replied the bishop, "Balaam could not speak himself; and so his ass spoke for him." (*The Annual Visitor, or Almanac, for...1801* (36842))

A certain noble Lord, one of Mr. Burke's supporters of his Corinthian pillar, asked a Clergyman, who dined with him, why a goose, if there was one, was always placed next to the Parson?—"Really" (said the Clergyman) "I can give no reason for it; but your question is so odd, that I shall never see a goose again without thinking of your Lordship." (*The Virginia and North Carolina Almanack for... 1801*(37046))

"Your unchristian virulence against me," said a Preacher, "may cost hundreds of people their lives!"—This alarming threat caused him to be brought before a Court of Justice: when it appeared, that if the people would not permit him to preach, he would turn Doctor! (*The Virginia and North Carolina Almanack for... 1801* (37046))

F. Heroic Clergymen

A clergyman of a facetious turn of mind, who lived in Sussex, a coast on which shipwrecks have frequently happened; and where, upon such occasions, the inhabitants, instead of assisting the unfortunates in their distress, used to plunder all they could lay hands on, and treat the people ill, and were so keen at the news of a wreck, that they would leave all manner of business to plunder. A misfortune of this kind, happening one *Sunday* during the time of divine service, the alarm was given, " *A Wreck! A Wreck!*" upon which they began to scamper out with great precipitation; which our parson perceiving, opened the pulpit door, and walking down the stairs, called out at the same time, with a loud voice, " *Brethren, let me intreat you to hear five words more.*" They turned about with impatient attention, to hear what the preacher had to say; who making hastily up to them, said, "Let us all start fair."—Which odd behavior had the desired effect; as he meant only to go with them, in order to prevent their abusing the ship's crew, which often happened. (*Hutchins Improved: Being an Almanack and Ephemeris...for...1781* (16807))

An Italian Bishop struggled through great difficulties without repining, and met with much opposition in discharge of his episcopal function without ever betraying the least impatience. An intimate friend of his, who admired those virtues which he thought it impossible to imitate, one day asked the prelate, if he could communicate the secret of being always easy? "Yes," (replied the old man,) "I can teach you my secret, and with great facility; it consists in nothing more than making a right use of my eyes." His friend begged him to explain himself. "Most willingly," (returned the Bishop,) "In whatever state I am, I first of all look up to Heaven, and remember that my principal business here, is to prepare for my journey there: I then look down upon the earth, and call to mind how small a space I shall occupy in it when I come to be interred: I then look abroad into the world, and observe what multitudes there are, who, in all respects, are more unhappy than myself. Thus I learn where true happiness is placed. Where all our care must end, and how very little reason I have to repine or complain." (*The Pennsylvania, New-Jersey, Delaware, Maryland and Virginia Almanac, for...1799* (34631))

Bishop B. who was a tall, strong, raw boned man, one Sunday preaching before the witty Earl of C. closed one of his sentences with a violent thump on the pulpit, which made the whole church ring, and this threatening interrogation, "Who dares deny what I say?"—"None," (said his Lordship) "who is within reach of that d—d large fist!" (*The Virginia and North Carolina Almanac, for...1800* (35239))

King James I of England once went out of his way to hear a noted preacher. The clergyman seeing the King enter, left his text to declaim against swearing, for which the King was notorious.—When done, James thanked him for his sermon, but asked what connection swearing had with it? He answered, "Since your Majesty came out of your way, I could not do less than go out of mine to meet you." (*The Gentlemen's and Ladies' Diary, and Almanac...for...1800* (35642))

G. The Children of Clergymen

Anecdote of Brigadier Ruggles
When he was a boy, he was sent by his father, who was the minister of the town where he lived, to fetch his horse from the pasture, for the minister of the adjacent town to examine, who wanted to purchase one. When he was returning, the minister who wanted to examine the horse, went privately to meet him, supposing he would be more likely to give an impartial account than his father would. The horse was very low in flesh, but very high spirited: "Your horse," says the minister, "appears to be heart whole, what makes him so poor?" "O," says the boy, "it fares with him as it does with about three fourths of the world, he has been d—dly priestridden." (*The New England Almanac...for...1797* (30308))

A clergyman seeing his son about to drink [   ] of brandy, says, "Son, don't drink that filthy stuff, ardent spirits is the worst enemy you have." "I know that, father," replied the son, "But you know we are commanded to love our enemies—so, here it goes." (*Poor Richard Revived: being the Farmer's Diary for ... 1797* (31099))

H. Catholic Clergy

Sometime before the abolition of the Jesuits, a gentleman in Paris died, and left all his estate from an only son then abroad, to that body of religious men, on condition that, on his return, the worthy fathers should give him—whatever they should *chuse.* When the son came home, he went to the convent, and received a very small share indeed. The wise sons of Loyola *chusing* to keep the greatest part to themselves. The young gentleman consulted his friends, and all agreed he was without remedy. At last a Barrister, to whom he happened to mention his case, advised him to sue the convent, and promised to gain him his cause. The gentleman followed his advice; and the suit terminated in his favor through the management of the advocate, who grounded his plea on this reasoning:—"The testator," says he, "has left his son that share of his estate, which the fathers should *chuse.* Now 'tis plain what part they have *chosen,* by what they keep to themselves. My client then stands on the words of the will.—'Let me have,' says he, ' *the part they have chosen, and I am satisfied.*' " It was accordingly awarded to him without hesitation. (*The United States Almanac, for ... 1800* (36599))

A Portugese sculptor, who had been suspected by the holy Fathers of the Church of the horrid sin of Free-thinking, lay at the point of death. A sanctified Jesuit, who came to confess him, holding up a Crucifix before his eyes, said, "Behold, sinful man, the God you have offended—Do you recollect him?"—"Yes, Father" (said the dying man) "I do recollect him; it was I who made him!" (*The Virginia and North Carolina Almanack for ... 1801* (37046))

A young woman, whose brother had embraced the Protestant religion, was convicted of having a bastard child, and obliged to do public penance. The priest, after a sharp reprimand, warned her that, as she had made a reparation for her own crime, she should never fall into her brother's. "Oh, Sir," said she, "I would rather commit my fault a thousand times, than be once guilty of his." (*An Astronomical Diary, Calendar, or Almanack, for ... 1801* (38550))

I. Miscellaneous Stories about Clergymen

A clergyman, dining or supping with a gentlewoman of the congregation, and a large uncut Cheshire cheese being brought upon the table, he asked her where he should cut, She replied, "Where you please, Sir." Upon which, he gave it to a servant in waiting, bade him carry it to his house, and he would cut it at home. (*Thomas's Massachusetts, Connecticut, Rhodeisland, Newhampshire and Vermont Almanack- ...for...1789* (21115))

A clergyman in Scotland, desired his hearers never to call one another liars; but, when one said the thing that was not, they ought to whistle.— On Sunday he preached a sermon on the parable of the loaves and fishes; and, being at a loss to explain it, he said that the loaves were not like those now-a-days, they were as big as some of the hills in Scotland. He had scarce pronounced these words, when he heard a loud whistle—"Who is that," (says he) "ca's me a liar?" "It is I, Whilly M'Donald, the baker." "Well Willey, what objections have ye to what I ha' told you?" "None, Mess John, only I want to know what sort of ovens they had to bake those loaves in." (*The American Almanac, for...1800* (35213))

Witchcraft
A Virginia Anecdote
About the year 1727, when the back settlers of that country were as proverbial for their prejudices, as ever the first settlers of Plymouth were, an old woman, about 120 miles from Richmond, on James river, was so unfortunate as to have a sow litter a pig with two tails. This circumstance soon overran the settlement. A general alarm was spread; and the parson of the parish was resorted to by the affrighted people to account for this wonderful phenomena: The sage divine, after duly considering the affair, declared that, as all pigs by *nature*, were endowed with one tail, it was probable that the *devil* was officious in the generation of this litter, and, as *he* cannot make any thing perfect, that these two tails were left as a mark of his imperfection; the parson further observed, that as other neighbours had sows, on whom the evil spirit might have tried his operations, his partiality to this old woman was a proof that she must have a connection with him, and that she could be nothing less than a *witch*. The poor woman was immediately apprehended, and it was determined to tie her up in a sack, and throw her into the river; if she floated she was a witch and must be *hung*, if she sunk she was *innocent*. A vast concourse of people assembled on the bank to see the operation, and while the church wardens were absolutely engaged in drawing the bag over her, a colonel Taylor, who was lately come from Ireland, hit on the following stratagem to save her.

"By my soul," said he to the wardens, "ye are all wrong; you know nothing of witches; now in Ireland, we have found out a much surer way, without half the trouble." The people were anxious to hear the Irish method, "Why" (says the colonel) "my jewels, we put the woman in one scale and the big church bible in the other; if the bible out weighs the woman she is a witch, and must be burned, but if the woman is the heaviest she is no witch by my soul." The colonel's method was approved of: the trial made, and thus the life of a woman preserved, who, but for Colonel Taylor's stratagem, must have fallen a sacrifice to the ignorance and prejudices of an illiterate people. (*Beers's Almanac for...1798* (31784))

A curate who had the honour to preach before the Bishop of D—acquited himself with great ease and self-possession. The prelate in conversing with him, enquired by what means he had acquired so much assurance, before so large an audience.—"I consider them as so many cabbages," replied the preacher. "But what do you think of me?" rejoined my lord. "As a colliflower amongst cabbages." He was not afterwards preferred. (*The Citizen and Farmer's Almanac, for...1801* (37185))

LAWYERS
A. Browbeating of Witnesses and Others

A humorous fellow, a carpenter, being subpoena'd as a witness on a trial for an assault; one of the counsel, who was very much given to browbeat the evidence, asked him what distance he was away from the parties when he saw the defendant strike the plaintiff? The carpenter answered, "Just four feet five inches and a half."

"Prithee, fellow," says the counsel, "how is it possible you can be so very exact as to the distance?"

"Why, to tell you the truth," says the carpenter, "I thought perhaps that some fool or other might ask me, so I measured it." (*Hutchin's Improved: Being an Almanack...for...1776* (14125))

The Lord Jeffries pleading at the bar, before he was made a Judge; a country fellow giving evidence against his client, pushed the matter very strongly: Jeffries, after his usual way, called out to the fellow, "Harkee, you fellow in the leather doublet, what have you for swearing?" "Faith, Sir," replied the countryman, "If you had no more for lying, than I have for swearing, you might e'en wear a leather doublet, too." (*The York, Cumberland and Lincoln Almanack, for...1788* (20467))

An arch prisoner, who had an unfavourable countenance, being brought to the bar to be tried for horse-stealing, the judge immediately cryed, "Oh, here is a noted villain, I'm sure? Why, sirrah, I can see the rogue in your face." "Ay, my Lord," says the fellow, "I wonder at that; for I did not know my face was a looking glass, till your Lordship saw yourself in it." (*Bickerstaff's New-England Almanack, for . . . 1792* (23986))

A countryman very much marked with the small pox, applied to a justice of the peace for redress in an affair where one of his neighbors had ill treated him; but not explaining the business so clearly as the justice expected, "Fellow," (said the justice in a rage) "I don't know whether you were innoculated for the small pox or not, but I am sure you have been for stupidity." "Why, and please you" (replied the man) "perhaps I might, as you say, be innoculated for stupidity, but there was no occasion to perform that upon your worship, for you seem to have had it the natural way." (*The American Almanac, for . . . 1801*(36808))

B. Impertinence Outside the Court

Three young lawyers riding from Bedford Court, across the Allegeny mountain, observed an old Dutch woman riding before them, with a leg on each side of a dull horse, whose sides she was pelting severely with her heels,—said one of them to the other, "I'll ride up and have some fun with her," and on riding up observed, to the woman, that her steed was very lazy. "Yes, pezure;" replied the old woman, "he is just like the lawyers; he will take a fee off both sides, and do very little after all." (*Father Tammany's Almanac for . . . 1793* (25059))

A little gentleman of the long robe, having a dispute with a remarkable bulky barrister, the big man threatened to put him in his pocket: "If you do," said Dapper, "You will have more law in your pocket, than ever you had in your head." (*The Pennsylvania, New-Jersey, Delaware, Maryland and Virginia Almanac, for . . . 1801* (38227))

C. Use of Jargon

An ordinary country fellow being called at an evidence in a court of judicature, in a cause where the terms mortgager and mortgagee were frequently used, the judge asked the countryman if he knew the difference between the mortgager and the mortgagee: "Yes," said he, "it is the same as between the nodder and the noddee," "How is that?" replied the judge. "Why you sit there," said the clown, "and I nod at you; then I am the nodder, and you the noddee." (*An Astronomical Diary or Almanack, for...1794* (26019))

A learned gentleman at the bar, when interrogating a sailor who was called as witness to a murder aboard a ship, asked him where the defendant was when he saw him strike the person murdered. "The defendant," (replied the sailor) "I don't know what you mean by the defendant." The counsellor argued that the sailor was not a competent witness, as he did not know what a plaintiff or defendant meant; however the sailor was suffered to proceed with his evidence, in the course of which he was asked by the aforesaid counsellor, in what part of the ship he stood when the fact was committed.— "Where did I stand," (replied the sailor with a sea-faring roughness) "why I stood abaft the binnacle!" "Abaft the binnacle!" (says the counsellor) "pray where is that?" "There is a pretty fellow of a counsellor," (replied the sailor) "who does not know where abaft the binnacle is!" (*The Town and Country Almanac, for...1799* (34545))

D. Cupidity of Lawyers

A stingy counsellor made a lady, to whom he made his addresses for marriage, pay very great fees; as she reproached him that he did not act gallantly.—"I had a mind," said he, "to convince you by your own experience, how lucrative the profession of counsellor is, in order to let you know I am a good match." (*Father Abraham's Almanack for...1779* (16050))

A counsel, not long since, in cross-examining a witness, asked him, among other questions—Where he was on a particular day:—to which he replied, he was in company with two friends—"Friends!" exclaimed the counsel, "two thieves I suppose you mean."—"They may be so," replied the witness, "for they are both lawyers." (*Poor Robin's Almanac, for...1792* (23076))

A tradesman of Windham, Connecticut, having occasion to boil a number of cattle's feet, threw the bones at the back of the Court-house. An attorney asked what bones they were? A bystander replied that he believed them to be *client's* bones, as they were well picked. (*Wheeler's North-American Calendar for...1793* (25027))

Some time in April last, Mr. Cowper, author of the Task, on his road to Lord Oxford's was followed and secured by some people at Barton Mills, who took him on suspicion that he was the noted Barrington, (a pick pocket) from the extraordinary length of his fingers. Mr. Cowper humoured the thing till he was carried to Lord Oxford's, at which place the matter was set right; and the countryman who secured him, was informed that he had mistaken his man, that the gentleman was a lawyer. &c, &c. "A lawyer!" said the disappointed rustic, "aye, aye, I thought those long fingers were not given him for nothing." (*Hodge's North-Carolina Almanack, for...1798* (32923))

One day a thief was carried to the gallows, and as his confessor asked him, whether he was not sorry for having committed the theft; "yes," he replied that he was, but more so on account of his not having stolen enough to bribe the judges. (*The Columbian Almanac: or, The North-American Calendar, for...1800* (35321))

Anecdote of Sir John Fielding
A fellow who made it his practice to pay sixpence for a bason of soup at various coffee houses, and steal at the same time a silver table spoon, was at last detected. Sir John Fielding asked him what he was? To which the gentleman replied, "I belong to the law, Sir." "The law, pshaw! that's impossible," said Sir John, "if you did, you would have stolen the bason, too." (*Farley and Goss' Almanac...for...1800* (35459))

E. Lawyers and Liars

In a cause lately tried in the Supreme Court (Pennsylvania) as the counsel were pointing out the boundaries of the land in question, on a map, one said, "We lie on this side;"—"and we," replied the other, "lie on this side." "If you *lie* on both sides," exclaimed a juryman, "whom are we to believe." (*An Astronomical Diary...for...1789* (21480))

As a minister and a lawyer were riding together, says the minister to the lawyer, "Sir, do you ever make any mistakes in pleading?" "I do," said the lawyer. "And what do you do with your mistakes?" "Why, sir, if large ones, I mend them: if small ones, I let them go," said the lawyer. "And pray, sir," said he "do you ever make any mistakes in preaching?" "Yes, sir, I do." "And what do you do with mistakes?" "Why, Sir, I dispense with them in much the same way you just observed: I rectify large ones, and neglect small ones. Not long since I went to observe that the devil was the father of liars, but mistook and said lawyers, and the mistake was so small I let it go." (*The Town and Country Almanack, for...1797* (31616))

A knavish attorney asking a very worthy gentleman, what Honesty was? " *What's that to you,*" said he, " *meddle with those things that concern you.*" (*The New-Jersey and Pennsylvania Almanac, for...1799* (34543))

F. Lawyers and the Devil

At a late court of Common Pleas in the Commonwealth of Massachusetts, the defendant said that if he lost the case he would appeal to the Supreme, and from there to the Federal Court and from there to Heaven. "Certainly, then," replied a gentleman, "you will be defaulted, not being present to answer yourself, and no attorney is ever admitted there." (Beers's Almanac...for...1793 (24083))

Epitaph on a Lawyer
Hic jacet Jacobus Straw,
Who forty years followed the law,
    When he dy'd,
    The devil cry'd
"John, give us you paw."
(Beers's Almanac...for...1794 (25152))

A grave old country blade coming before a judge and taking his oath on a cause, he was bid to have a care what he swore to, lest he went to the devil. "I fear not that," replied he, by way of retort, "for I have given him my oldest son, and he ought to be content with one out of a family." "How's that?" says the judge; "Pray explain yourself." " *Why, truly, I have made him a lawyer, and you know the devil was a lawyer from the beginning.*" "A liar, you mean," says the other. "I know not," replied he, "what distinction there may be in *town*, but I am sure, by sad experience, *we in the country know no difference between a lawyer and a liar.*" (The Farmer's Almanack...for...1797 (31294))

A country attorney happening to be at a tavern with an honest peasant, and was very facetious at the countryman's expense. They nevertheless agreed to try for a bottle of wine who could make the best rhyme. The lawyer enquired the peasant's occupation, who cheerfully informed him he was a weaver, upon which the lawyer wrote the lines:

    The world, tho' large, is but a span;
    It takes nine weavers to make one man.
The weaver in his turn, enquired the lawyer's occupation, and being informed: "I thought," said he, "you were of the law by the glibness of your tongue, but since you have rhymed about the world, so will I too," and then he wrote,
    The world is wide, and full of evil,
    And half a lawyer makes a devil.

(*Croswell's Diary: or The Catskill Almanack, for...1800* (35165))

An attorney observed a boy about nine years of age, diverting himself at play, whose eccentric appearance attracted his attention, "Come here my lad," said he. The boy accordingly came, and after chatting a bit, asked the attorney what case was to be tried next. "A case between the Pope and the devil," (answered the attorney), "and which do you suppose will gain the action?" "I don't know," said the boy, "I guess 'twill be a pretty tight squeeze; the Pope has the most money, but the devil has the most lawyers." (*The New-England Almanack for...1801* (37279))

G. Virtuous Lawyers and Justices

Serjeant Maynard, an eminent counsellor of the last century, waiting with the body of the law upon the Prince of Orange (afterwards King William) at his arrival in London, the Prince took notice of his great age, the Serjeant being then near ninety. "Sir," (said he,) "you have outlived all the men of the law of your younger years."

"I should have outlived even the law itself," replied the Serjeant, "if your Highness had not come over." (*Father Abraham's Almanack, for...1778* (15576))

On a Lawyer
God works wonders now and then,
Here lies a Lawyer, an honest man.
(*The New-England Callendar: or Almanack, for...1793* (25026))

Four qualities are requisite in a good judge; to hear with patience, to answer with prudence, to condemn with justice, and execute with mercy, for he that is impatient in hearing, indifferent in answering, partial in sentencing, and cruel in executing, deserves rather to be arraigned for his own crimes than to judge those of others. (*An Astronomical Diary, or Almanac, for...1799* (34529))

Of Sir Thomas Moor
When he was Lord Chancellor, he decreed a gentleman to pay a sum of money to a poor widow, whom he had wronged; to whom the gentleman said, "Then I hope your Lordship will grant me a long day to pay it:"—"I will grant your motion," said the Chancellor; "Monday next is St. Barnabas's day, which is the longest day in the year; pay it the widow that day, or I will commit you to the Fleet." (*Greenleaf's New-York, Connecticut, and New-Jersey Almanack, for...1800* (35170))

A poor fellow condemned to be hung, told the late Judge Burnet, it was a very hard thing to be hung for stealing a horse, "No, friend," said the Judge, "You are not hanged for stealing a horse, but that horses may not be stolen." (*Curtis's Pocket Almanack for...1801* (37275))

H. Miscellaneous Stories about Lawyers and Justices

He that would go to Law, must have a good Cause--a heavy Purse— a skillful Attorney—an able Advocate—good Evidence—an intelligent jury— upright and patient Judges—and having all these, unless he has very good Luck, he will stand but a small Chance of succeeding in his Suit. (*An Astronomical Diary...for...1788* (20466))

A Justice of the Peace, remarked to a Clergyman who rode an elegant horse, that he was prouder than his master. "Why really, Sir," retorted the Parson; "so many *asses* have been converted of late, into Justices, that I could not find one to ride upon." (*The Farmer's Almanack...for...1793* (24847))

A student of the Middle Temple being just called to the bar, sent for the peruke maker to measure him for a new tye wig. The perriquier in applying his apparatus in one direction, was observed to smile: upon which the young barrister desiring to know what ludicrous circumstance gave rise to his mirth; the barber replied, that he could not help remarking the extreme *length* of his honour's head. "That's well," (said the student) "we lawyers have occasion for *long heads*." The barber, who by this time had completed the dimensions, now burst out into a fit of laughter; and an explanation being insisted on, at last declared, that he could not possibly contain himself, when he discovered that his honour's head was just as *thick* as it was *long*. (*Hodge's North-Carolina Almanack, for...1798* (32923))

Not long since, a milkman, in passing through one of the streets in Dublin, laid down his milk-pail in order to take a glass with a friend at a public house; in the mean time, a thirsty ass happened to pass by, had sense enough to avail himself of the opportunity, and in a few minutes drank the whole with as much ease as a common councilman would drain a tankard of Calvert's entire or Whitbread's royal porter. The milkman immediately hurried the ass before a magistrate who did not fail to hail his brother in one of the most musical notes he was master of; this, of course, drew the attention of the dispenser of justice, who listened to the story with uncommon patience; he was candid enough, however to acknowledge, that as the case was new he should reserve it for the opinion of his brethren; at last he bethought himself of a cobler that used to assist him in many points [   ] made his appearance, and having heard the whole, he only wished to ask one question—"Pray was the ass sitting or standing?" "Standing:" "Well, Mr. Milkman, you must put up with your loss: for it is a rule in all our clubs that no man ever pays for a standing drink." "If that is the case," said the plaintiff, "I shall take care [not] to bring one ass before another as long as I live again." (*The Virginia Almanac, for...1798* (33131))

A notorious thief, being to be tried for his life, confessed the robbery he was charged with. The judge hereupon directed the jury to find him guilty, upon his own confession. The jury having laid their heads together, brought him in not guilty. The judge bid them consider of it again; but still they brought in their verdict, not guilty. The judge asked them the reason: the foreman replied, "there is reason enough, *for we all know him to be one of the greatest liars in the world.*" (*Franklin's Legacy: or, The New-York and Vermont Almanack, for...1799* (34376))

"Silence! keep silence in the court," said, one day, an angry judge, "why will you not keep silence? Here we have judged a dozen causes this morning, and have not heard a word of one of them." (*The United States Almanac, for...1801* (36934))

PHYSICIANS
A physician being asked the best way to preserve health, answered, "keep the feet warm, the head cool, and the belly, open, then a fig for the doctor." (*Father Tammany's Almanac, for...1787* (20160))

The late Earl of Chatham, who bore no good will to a certain physician, was rallying him one day about the inefficacy of his prescriptions. To which the Doctor replied, "He desired any of his patients to find fault with him." "I believe you," (replied the witty Earl)—"FOR THEY ARE ALL DEAD." (*The Virginia Almanack, for...1788* (20199))

Like a prompt sculler, one Physician plies,
And all his force, and all his physic tries.—
But two physicians, like a pair of oars,
Conduct you soonest to the stygian shores.
(*The Burlington Almanac, for...1791* (22384))

Sir Charles Wager, was seized with a fever, while upon a cruize. He was blooded and blistered. The doctor then recommended a few boluses and pills. "No, no, avast there," cried the old sea man, "batter my hulk, if you please, but by Jove, you shan't board me." (*Stoddard's Diary: or, the Columbia Almanack, for...1791* (22595))

One of the bar, and another of the medical tribe, having a dispute about precedence, left it to Diogenes who gave it in preference of the long robe, by observing, the thief might go before, and the executioner follow. (*Beers's Almanac...for...1793* (24083))

A gentleman calling upon a friend in London who was attended by a physician from the west end of town, enquired of the doctor, on one of his visits, if he did not find it very inconvenient to attend his friend from such a distance?—"Not at all, Sir," replied the doctor, "for having another patient in the adjoining street, I can KILL two birds with one stone." "Can you so," replied the sick man, "then you are too good a shot for me," and dismissed him. (*The Virginia Almanack, for...1793* (24970))

A surgeon of a ship who used in every disease to prescribe them salt water was returning from shore, the rope by which he ascended by some accident broke, and the surgeon fell into the water, on which bawling out lustily one of the sailors inquired, "What's the matter." "Why," answered a messmate, "the Doctor has only fallen into his medicine chest." (*An Astronomical Diary, or Almanack, for...1796* (29493))

An Irish surgeon who had couched a cataract and restored the sight of a poor woman in Dublin, observed in her case what he deemed a phaenomenon in optics; on which he called together his professional brethren, declaring himself unequal to the solution.

He stated to them that the sight of his patient was so perfectly restored, that she could see to thread the smallest needle, or to perform any other operation, which required particular accuracy of vision; but that when he presented her with a book, she was not capable of distinguishing one letter from another!

This very singular case excited the ingenuity of all the gentlemen present, and various solutions were offered, but none could command the general assent. Doubt crowded on doubt, and the problem grew darker from every explanation, when at length, by a question put by the servant who attended, it was discovered that the woman never learned to read! (*The United States Almanac, for...1798* (32296))

The Arcanum of the College

"My father desired me, sir to *ax* you," said a physical disciple to a certain eminent pharmacopolist, "that I might attend you to all your patients, as you know, sir, it is the last year of my time"—"You shall, Bob, you shall," replied the master; "Come get your hat."—They entered the sick man's chamber—and the usual circumstances occurred, such as feeling the pulse, *et cetera*. After assuming an appearance of profound thought, the vender of galenicals told the wife of the sick man, with much gravity, that her husband was in extreme danger, and that she had contributed to his malady by giving him oysters. The woman imagined the apothecary dealt with the devil, and [   ] owned the fact.—When they had quitted the [house] Bob inquired with much earnestness of his master, how he could possibly know that the patient had [eat]en oysters,—"You foolish boy," replied the other. [I saw the shells] under the bed.—The next time [Bob went alone] and returned with a ghastly vissage, [for] the patient was dead [from having eaten a horse].—"A horse, Bob," rejoined the Esculapian chief, "[How] do you know that?" "Oh, easy enough sir, I looked under the bed, and saw a bridle and saddle!" (*The Virginia Almanac, for. . .1798* (33131))

A foolish idle fellow, at Florence (Italy) hearing that a physician had obtained great wealth and credit by the sale of some pills, undertook to make pills himself, and to sell them. He administered the same pills to all persons whatever; and as, by chance, they sometimes succeeded, his name became famous. A countryman called on him, and desired to know if his pills would enable him to find an ass he had lately lost. The quack bade him swallow six pills. In his way home, the operation of the pills obliged him to retire into a wood, where he found his ass. The clown, in consequence, spread a report, that he knew a doctor who sold pills that would recover *strayed cattle. (Franklin's Legacy: or, The New-York and Vermont Almanack, for. . .1799* (34376))

A physician was asked, whether his patient's fever had gone off? "I believe so," answered the Doctor, "and the man is gone with it." (*Isaiah Thomas's Massachusetts, Connecticut, Rhodeisland, Newhampshire and Vermont Almanack. . .for. . .1799* (34652))

A physician observed to a clock maker whose work needed mending, that if he was to make such errors in practice, it would be attended with the loss of all his patients. The man drily replied—"Good Doctor, the *Sun* discovers my faults—the *earth* hides yours." (*Isaiah Thomas's Massachusetts, Connecticut, Rhodeisland, Newhampshire and Vermont Almanack-. . .for. . .1799* (34652))

POLITICIANS

A. Getting Votes

The Power of Love, Mirth, and Money

The ingenious Sir Richard Steele, represented the borough of Stockbridge, in the county of Hants, in Parliament; and though he was powerfully opposed in his election, yet he had a great majority of votes: by a strategem which made all women of his side. Having made a great entertainment for the burgesses and their wives, and after having been very free and facetious, he took up a large apple, and sticking it full of guineas, declared it should be the prize of that man, whose wife should be first brought to bed after that day nine months. This afforded a great deal of mirth; and that with the entertainment, and the hopes of getting the prize, the good women prevailed upon their husbands to vote for Sir Richard, whom they to this day commemorate, and, it is said, once made a strong push to get a standing order of the corporation made, that no man should be accepted as a candidate for that Borough, who did not offer himself upon the same terms. (*Beers's Almanac...for...1797* (30044))

Not long since, two gentlemen, Mr. B.D. and Mr. H.L. stood candidates for a seat in one of our Legislatures. They were violently opposed to each other—however, by some artifice or other, Mr. D. got the election—when he was returning home much elated with his success, he met a gentleman, an acquaintance of his—"Well," says D. "I have got the election—L. was no match for me—I'll tell you how I flung him—If there happened any Dutch votes, I could talk Dutch to them, *and there I had the advantage of him*—If there were any Frenchmen I could talk French with them, *and there I had the advantage of him*—But as for L., he was a clever, honest, sensible little fellow." "Yes Sir," replied the gentleman, *"and there he had the advantage of you."* (*The New-England Almanac...for...1799* (33595))

The Humorous Cobler

A candidate for a seat in parliament, who to gain a temporary popularity in a small borough, practised every mean condescension, was informed that nothing could tend more to secure his election than the winning over of a certain cobler, who, what with his relations amongst the voters, and the facetiousness of his humour had a very considerable interest. He accordingly applied to him for his favour; when the cobler said, "Kiss me, and then I'll readily talk with you." This was immediately complied with. "Now," continued the cobler, "if for the sake of a few votes, you would kiss the begrimed face of such a dirty low-lived blackguard as I am, I make no doubt, but for a place or a pension you would kiss any smooth courtier's backside; so my very slabbering friend, you have no vote of mine I promise you." (*Beers' Almanac for...1801* (36924))

B. Hypocrisy of Politicians

A gentleman, not remarkable for his steadiness to a party, was complaining that he was troubled with *a pain in his side*; "Sir," said a friend, "when you find yourself uneasy *on one side*, you have nothing to do but *turn to the other.*" (*An Astronomical Diary, or Almanac for...1793* (24781))

One said that Watermen might be taken for Politicians, because they look one way and row another. (*Anderson Revived, for...1795* (26566))

C. Parties

On Parties
Both make the public good their pies,
The end of all their wishes;
With half an eye a man may see,
Both want the loaves and fishes.
(*Banneker's Wilmington Almanac, for...1795* (26613))

D. Foolish Speeches

A young member of the house of Commons was tempted to display his oritorial abilities, by the success and applause with which some eloquent members were attended; accordingly, on a certain subject, he rose up with great importance, and said, "Mr. Speaker, have we laws or have we not laws? if we have laws and they are not obeyed, for what purpose were these laws made?" After he was seated some time, another member rose and said, "Mr. Speaker, did the honorable gentleman who spoke last, speak to the purpose, or did he not speak to the purpose? If he did not speak to the purpose, to what purpose did he speak?" (*The Kentucky Almanac, for...1798* (32338))

A member of a certain Legislature, who indulged himself in afternoon naps, requested his friend to awaken him when the Lumber Bill came on. He omitted it by forgetfulness, but finally gave him a jog, as the House was discussing a bill to prevent *Fornication.*—Old Sleepy-Head started, rubbed his eyes, and exclaimed: "Mr. Speaker! Mr. Speaker! a word or two upon this bill, for half my constituents get their living no other way." *(The Newport Almanac, for...1800* (35969))

E. Dishonesty Among Politicians

About fifty years ago, the General Assembly of New Hampshire used to set in a tavern. A countryman happened to come into Portsmouth to buy *nails,* and was enquiring at the shop for *single-tens.* A waggish fellow, known by the name of Doctor Moses, over-hearing him, directed him to the tavern, where he told him were plenty of single-tens. The man went, and enquired of two members, who happened to be in the porch—they deemed it an insult on the house and made a complaint to the speaker. The man was taken into custody, and laid the blame on Moses. He was then sent for, and having acknowledged the fact, was ordered to receive the speaker's reprimand and ask pardon on *his knees.* Moses obeyed, and having performed his humiliation, as he was rising from the floor, brushed his knees with his hand, and exclaimed, " *a dirty house! a dirty house!"* (*The Virginia Almanack, for... 1791* (22315))

A member of the Boston Assembly, some years ago, vexed at something that had passed in the house, left it in a pet, declaring that not one of the members was fit to carry *offals* to a bear: the members being informed of this uncouth speech sent word to the culprit, that as he had spoken in a very disrespectful manner of the house, they would not permit him to take his seat again, unless he would unsay what he had said, acknowledge that he was sorry and beg their pardon. The offender made his appearance without hesitation, and upon entering said, "Gentlemen of this honourable house, being told that your honours are much incensed at an observation I made and that I could only atone for my fault by making certain concessions, I now comply, (falling upon his knees)—Whereas I said not one of you was fit to carry offals to a bear: I now unsay it, and declare that you are *every one* very well qualified for that office—I ask your pardon, and am *very sorry for it*: but really," (added he, rising and wiping the dust from his knees) "I think *this* is as *dirty a house* as ever I *met with."* (*An Almanack...for...1794* (25850))

As a country gentleman in London was reading a newspaper in a Coffee-house, he said to a friend who sat next him, "I have been looking for some time to see what the ministry are about, but I cannot find where those articles are put, not being used to the London papers."—" *Look among the robberies,"* replied the other. (*The Newhampshire and Vermont Almanac, for...1795* (27379))

F. Miscellaneous Stories about Politicians

The members of a certain legislative body in one of the United States are remarkable for being mostly fat, corpulent men, and what the French call Bon Vivants (good livers). A stranger being one day introduced to hear their debates, a gentleman whispered. "You now see, sir, collected in one body the WISDOM OF THE LAND." "Faith," replied the other, "from the appearance of most of them, I should rather take them to be the FAT OF THE LAND." (*The Virginia Almanack, for...1792* (23125))

A niggarly representative, taking advantage of privilege, past over Charles River without paying toll. The toll man calls after him, "Sir, your copper." The representative replied, "I belong to the house." "Do you," (says the wit) "I really thought you belonged to the barn." (*The Middlesex Almanack...for...1792* (23808))

At the conclusion of a meeting, for choice of town officers, a Mr. Shote was chosen hog constable; which produced the subsequent impromptu:
The wisdom of the town now stands confest,
One *Shote* is chose to govern all the rest. (*An Astronomical Diary...for...1793* (24825))

Chapter Seven
Soldiers and Sailors

Early American almanac humor often expressed ambivalent attitudes toward military and naval figures. America, as many of the stories in Chapter One show, felt gratitude toward her own military heroes including such generals as Putnam, Washington and Gates. On the other hand, America felt that the Europeans often engaged in military excess. Washington's Farewell Address, which warns against the dangers of a standing army reflects one side of the American feeling about the military. The other side, of course, was represented by Washington's overwhelming victories in the first elections for the American presidency.

Almanac humor which deals with soldiers and sailors represents the ambivalent attitudes of Americans. Chapter One shows several stories about heroic soldiers. In this chapter there are several stories about both heroic and other kinds of soldiers and sailors. Soldiers often considered themselves above the law. They often saw their own fighting as an end in itself rather than as subordinate to a national cause. Some soldiers are made fun of for carrying the idea of courage to a ridiculous point.

Sailors in the almanac humor shared many of the characteristics of soldiers, but there was less emphasis on their role as fighters, much less emphasis on the role of officers and more emphasis on the common sailor as a drinker, a plain-speaker and, sometimes a fool. The term "sailor," of course, unlike "soldier" refers to both merchant sailors and naval sailors. Less emphasis on the sailors' role as fighters is probably to be expected.

SOLDIERS

A. Courage and Lack of Courage

Sobieski, King of Poland, getting upon his horse to succor Vienna, perceived the Queen bathed in a flood of tears, having at her side the prince her son who was very little. The King asked the princess the cause of her grief; "It is," answered she, "because the prince is too young to follow you." (*Father Abraham's Almanack for . . . 1779* (16050))

136

A soldier was bragging before Julius Caesar, of the wounds he had received in his face. Caesar, knowing him to be a coward, told him, he had best take heed the next time he ran away, *how he looked back.* (*Father Hutchins Revived for...1793* (24416))

A gentleman named Ball, being about to purchase a cornetcy in a regiment of horse, was presented to the colonel for approbation, who being a nobleman, declared he did not like the *name* and would have no *Balls* in his regiment. "Nor *Powder*," said the gentleman, "if your Lordship could help it." (*Anderson Revived, for...1795* (26566))

A Gascon soldier being asked by one of his comrades, as they were marching to an attack, What made him tremble? " *Why*," said he, "my body *trembles when it thinks of the heroic acts to which my Soul will drive it.*" (*Greenleaf's New York, Connecticut and New Jersey Almanack- ...for...1796* (28251))

A fellow hearing the drums beat up for volunteers for France, in the expedition against the Dutch, imagined himself valiant enough, and thereupon listed himself; returning again, he was asked by his friends, what exploits he had done there? He said, that he had cut off one of the enemies' legs: And being told that it had been more honourable and manly to have cut off his head: "Oh!" said he, *"you must know that his head was cut off before.*" (*The New-England Almanac...for...1798* (32012))

On the evening before a battle, an officer came to his General, to ask permission to go see his father, who he said was at the point of death, in order that he might pay his last duty to him. "Go," replied the General, who well knew that *cowardice* was the cause of the request, "honor thy father and thy mother, *that thy days may be long in the land.*" (*Croswell's Diary: or, The Catskill Almanack, for...1800* (35165))

B. The Purpose of the Military

A soldier in the late war had stolen a shirt from a farmer, to whom he would not make restitution.—"Well," (said the farmer) "if you keep it, you will pay for it in this world or the next."—"Faith," replied the soldier, "if you will trust so long, I will take another." (*Thomas's Massachusetts, Connecticut, Rhode-Island, Newhampshire and Vermont Almanack- ...for...1791* (22537))

When Christian, Duke of Brunswick, was employed in the siege of Leipsic, his army lay encamped in the vicinity of a rich monastery. In a case of sudden exigence, he requested the friars to assist his present necessities either by money or provisions, promising faithfully to repay them. As he was a Protestant, they, under pretence of poverty, refused his request—and he had in vain endeavored to negotiate a loan with some distant bankers. The Duke, in great anger, went in person, with a detachment of soldiers, and took possession of the monastery. Upon entering the chapel, he saw images of the twelve Apostles, and of divers other Saints, in massy silver. The Duke asked certain of the friars who those old-fashioned gentlemen were? They answered, "the twelve Apostles." "The twelve Apostles!" exclaimed the Duke, "why they were ordered to go abroad amongst [   ] nations, and ought not to be detained here as prisoners." So without hesitation he commanded them to be taken down, and coined into [   ]-dollars for the use of his troops. (*Beers's Almanac...for...1797* (30044))

In almost all religious wars the contending powers have occasionally offered up prayers to heaven for their own success, and the extirpation of their enemies; and each party have generally added, according to the justness of our cause, O Lord! help us &c. Considering that the cause of both parties cannot be precisely just, it would perhaps be quite as judicious, and somewhat more modest, to adopt the language, or at least the spirit of an old Scotch woman who was a sutler in the Duke of Marlborough's army. It so happened that this faithful follower of the camp was one evening talking to a venerable sister of the same profession, but not of the same country, on the probable consequences of an engagement expected to be fought between the two armies the next morning. "Well," says the English sutler, "well—it will certainly be a most bloody battle, and all I have to say is, may God stand by the right." "De'el pick out your eyne for your wicked wish," replied the Scotch one, "God stand by Hamilton's regiment, right or wrang!" (*The Citizen and Farmer's Almanac, for...1801* (37185))

C. Military Honor and Customs

A recruiting serjeant beating up in Birmingham sometime since, said in his fine speech—"As a further encouragement for recruits to enter, you shall have

Six pence a day,

As long as you stay."

To which a shrewd by-stander added, "And a thousand lashes if you go away." (*An Astronomical Diary, or Almanac, for...1793* (24781))

A military gentleman in Paris lately invited much company to dinner. His son, six years old, came to the table, but was repulsed, and told that *his beard was too short to dine with his father.* The mother, as much mortified as her son, made up a little side table for him, and ordered that he should be well attended. A large cat, however, repeatedly tried to take away his victuals, on which the child, out of all patience, exclaimed, " *go and eat with my papa. You have a beard long enough.*" (*Stoddard's Diary: or the Columbia Almanack, for...1797* (30048))

At the siege of Charleston, an American soldier had been bribed to convey to the enemy a plan and state of the works, ammunition, &c. After he had passed the lines, he was discovered by the piquette; who having repeatedly called on him to return, were at length obliged to fire at him and wounded him so he could not proceed. Upon examining the papers with which he was charged, they were found so accurately and ingeniously executed, that general Lincoln was convinced they were the work of another hand, and offered the soldier his life, provided he would discover the person in the garrison who had employed him. This offer was rejected, with an observation, that he knew the risk which accompanied his attempt, and had received an adequate consideration. The usual arrangements were, therefore, made for his execution, and the rope being tied about his neck, the general hoped that such circumstances would have shaken his fortitude, and sent an aid-de-camp to make another tender of pardon upon the same terms. "No!" exclaimed the resolute victim, "you have my life in your power, but my honour is my own." The signal was immediately given; he was consigned to eternity under the impression of his noble sentiment; and it is remarkable, that the hangman, as he descended from his duty, was killed by a shot from the British piquette. Such conduct, however, proves the inconsistency of the human character; nor is it easy to conceive, how a mind, so solicitous to preserve its dignity in a matter merely personal, should have condescended to engage in treachery. (*The Farmer's Almanac, for...1800* (35460))

A general of Frederick II King of Prussia, commisioned by his master to purchase certain maps, went to a print-seller's shop for that purpose. "Sir," said the shop-keeper, "do you want provincial maps or general ones?"—"Blood and thunder," replied the indignant man of war, "don't you see the plume in my hat, and does not that inform you that I am a general, and that consequently I must have general maps? Would you give me then the maps of an ensign or a pitiful lieutenant? Learn better how to speak to a person of my rank." (*The United States Almanac, for...1800* (36599))

D. Foolish Soldiers

A German peasant, newly enlisted in the army, was scarcely arrived at the regiment when he was sent with others upon a skirmishing party; and approaching a wood from whence the musket balls flew pretty thick, he stepped out of his rank, and making a sign for the enemy to desist, at the same time exclaimed, "Why what the devil are you about, don't you see there are people a coming." (*Beers's Almanac for...1801* (36924))

A soldier in the last wars, a little before an engagement found a horse shoe, and stuck it into his belt; shortly after, in the heat of the action, a bullet came and hit him upon that part. "Well," said he, "I find a little armour will serve a turn, if it be put in the right place." (*Bickerstaff's Genuine Almanack, for...1798* (33200))

E. Miscellaneous Stories about Soldiers

At the seige of Bonel, in 1599, there happened a singular case, and perhaps the only one in its kind. Two brothers, who had never seen, and had always been inquiring after the other, met at last by chance at that siege, where they served in two different companies. The elder who was called Hernando Diaz, having heard the other mentioned by the name of Enciero, which was his mother's surname, and which he had taken through affection, a thing pretty common in Spain, put several questions to him concerning a number of family particulars, and knew at last by the exactness of his answers that he was the brother he had so long been seeking after; whereupon both proceeding to a close embrace, a cannon ball struck off their heads, without separating their bodies, which fell clung together. Thus died these two brothers at the most agreeable time of their life. (*Bickerstaff's New-England Almanack for...1776* (14066))

During Benedict Arnold's military operations in Virginia, he took an American captain prisoner. After some general conversation with the captain, he asked him what he thought the Americans would do with him if they caught him?" The captain at first declined giving him an answer: but upon being repeatedly urged to it he said, "Why, sir, if I must answer your question, you must excuse my telling you the plain truth: if my countrymen should catch you, I believe they would first cut off that lame leg* which was wounded in the cause of freedom and virtue, and bury it with the honours of war, and afterwards hang the remainder of your body in gibbetts."

*Alluding to the wound he received in one of his legs at the attack upon Quebec. (Beers's note) (*Beers's Almanack...for...1792* (23163))

An officer in the late war journeying through a country town stopped at a tavern; being seated by the fire, he entered into conversation with an elderly gentleman, who by his discourse, convinced the officer that he was no fool of a mathematician. "Pray, Sir," says the officer, "as you appear to be a great scholar, can you tell me how long it would take me to surmount an insurmountable difficulty." "Yes," replied the old man, "just as long as it will take you to fall into a bottomless pit." "Faith," says the officer, "that's too deep for me," and made off as fast as he could. (*The Farmer's Almanack for...1794* (26254))

An old continental arrived at an inn, and asked for refreshment. The hostess set before him a bone of ham, and crust of bread. Her son, who had been an officer, gave the poor fellow a shilling, when he had done picking, and bid him march off. Soon after the old woman comes in to look for her pay. "Mother," says the officer, "what might the picking of that bone be worth?"—"Why, about one and six pence, these hard times." "Well," cries the humane son, "I have made a fine bargain, and saved six pence, for I gave him but a shilling to pick the whole." (*Phinney's Calendar or Western Almanac for...1801* (36933))

SAILORS

A. Courage and Lack of Courage

Anecdote of a Brave Gunner at Minorca

In the sea fight off Minorca in 1756, a gunner had his right hand shot away just as he was going to fire a gun; when the brave fellow, taking up the match, clapped it to the touch hole saying, quite unconcerned, "So you thought I had but one arm." (*An Astronomical Ephemeris, Kalendar, or Almanack, for...1776* (14479))

A lieutenant, having deserted his post in the late naval engagement, at one time lay flat on the deck in all the agonies of fear.—Such a circumstance, it is in the recollection of many, occurred in the war before last. The surgeon observed it, told the sailors that the Lieutenant was mortally wounded, ordered them to throw him overboard. The culprit struggled stupidly against the sentence and declared himself unhurt. The tars asked him gravely, "whether he should know better than the surgeon?" and executed their directions, to a letter! (*The United States' Almanac...for...1797* (30437))

A sea officer, who, for his courage in a former engagement, where he had lost his leg, had been preferred to the command of a good ship; in the heat of the next engagement, a cannon ball took off his wooden deputy, so that he fell upon the deck; a seaman, thinking he had been fresh wounded, called out for a surgeon, "No, no," said the captain, "the carpenter will do." (*The Kentucky Almanac, for...1797* (30658))

B. Insolent Sailors

In a great storm at sea when all expected to be cast away, they went to prayers; in the midst of their devotion, a boy falls a laughing. The Captain asked him what he meant by it—"Why truly Sir," said he, "I laugh at that man's fiery nose there, to think what a hissing it will make by and by, when it comes into the water." (*Beers's Almanac...for...1794* (25152))

A gentleman who was very crooked, was met in the road by a sailor who asked him if he came straight from home, and was replied to in the affirmative—"Then," says the sailor, "your honour was very much warp'd by the way." (*Poor Richard Revived: being the Farmer's Diary for...1797* (31099))

A stranger passing St. Paul's Church, asked a tar, whom he met, what those figures were at the west front. To which the sailor answered, "the twelve apostles." "How the devil can that be," replied the other, "when there are but six of them?" "D—n my eyes," says the tar, "would you have them all upon deck at once?" (*Franklin's Legacy: or, The New-York and Vermont Almanack, for...1799* (34376))

A sailor passing one of the wharves in Boston, with a coil of rope on his arm, was accosted by a shopkeeper, who was standing by his door, with, "My lad, that rope is not fixed on the right place." "I know that," replied the sailor, "if it was, it would be round your neck." (*The Farmer's Almanack, for...1799* (34968))

C. Drunken Sailors

The Sailor

When on a gunnel of a ship,
Poor Jack was funning with some flip,
There came a cruel cannon Ball,
Which shot his foot off, leg and all.
Jack saw his expectations crost,
And cry'd, "D—n me, the flip is lost."
(*Strong's Astronomical Diary, Calendar, or Almanack, for...1797* (31248))

A poor drunken sailor being asked, if he was sure of being gratified three wishes, what would they be, replied—"My first would be *all* the brandy in the world." "Your next Jack?" "All the tobacco in the world." "Now for the third"—"Why d—n my eyes, *more* brandy." (*Beers's Almanac for...1800* (35164))

D. Miscellaneous Stories about Sailors

An old Sea Captain fond of having good helmsmen, never entered any sailor, without declaring THAT HE MUST STEER THRO A MUSQUETOE'S EYE. One of the crew, at first taking the wheel, was near broaching the ship too, and then gave her a yaw off full of wild. The Captain came storming upon deck. "Sir," says the fellow, "I was LOOKING FOR THE MOSQUETOE'S EYE, TO GO THRO' IT NEXT TURN." (*An Almanack, for...1794* (25260))

A sailor falling out of the main-top of a man of war, by great good luck, fell plump on his breech unhurt, and looking about him, seemingly unconcerned, as if nothing had happened, cry'd, "Blast my eyes, what a move that was." (*The Kentucky Almanac, for...1797* (30658))

As George the Third, was walking the quarter deck, with his hat on, a sailor asked his messmate, who that sailor was, that did not [dowse] his peak to the Admiral? "Why, the King," says Jack—"Well, King or no King," retorts the other, "he is an unmannerly dog." "Lord, where should he learn manners?" replies Jack," *he never was out of sight of land in his life.*" (*Isaiah Thomas's Massachusetts, Connecticut, Rhodeisland, Newhampshire and Vermont Almanack...for...1799* (34652))

A sea captain having just come ashore, was invited by some gentlemen to a hunting match. After the sport was over, he gave his friends this particular account of the pastime he had: "Our horses being completely rigged. We manned them, and the wind being at the south west twenty of us being in company, away we set over the Downs. In the time of half a watch we spied a bate under full gale: we tacked and stood after her; coming up on her, she tacked and we tacked upon which tack I had like to have run aground—but getting close off, I stood after her again: but as the devil would have it, being just about to lay her aboard, bearing too much wind, I and my horse overset, and came keel upwards." (*The United States Almanac, for...1801* (36934))

Sailing on Land—an humorous disaster

A British sailor, some time ago, having occasion to take a journey of ten or twelve miles into the country hired a horse for that purpose; and, having never been on horseback before, he asked one of his messmates how he should conduct himself. The latter told him, all that he had to do was to take care the horse did not *run away with him*. The other began to consider how he should avoid such a miscarriage, and at last hit on a scheme for that purpose. He took a small anchor, belonging to one of the [boats,] and having [tied] ten or twelve fathoms of rope to it, he [tied] one end of the rope about the horse's neck, and took the anchor up before him, to be ready for casting in case of any disaster.—The horse went very well for the first four or five miles, till, feeling himself galled by the rubbing of the anchor on his neck, he set off full speed; and our Equestrian finding himself in danger, determined to *bring up*. He therefore let go of the anchor; and the horse having run out his cable, *brought up* with such a jerk, that he threw his rider five or six yards before him, dislocating his shoulder and cured him effectually of any wish to make further improvements in the art of sailing on land. (*An Astronomical Diary, Calendar, or Almanack, for . . . 1799* (34616))

Chapter Eight
A Miscellany of Stories and Diversions

Many other stories appeared in American almanacs between 1776 and 1800. Hundreds of them either do not fall into categories or fall into such small categories that they cannot be assigned a chapter of their own. A fairly large category of stories about historical figures from Europe is also included by a very small representation in this chapter. Such stories, at least for modern American readers, tend to be long and dull. A few of the best have been selected so that a general representation of all almanac humor can be presented.

Several of the comic items in this chapter are of some importance to the development of American humor. Several of the stories have reappeared in more American forms. The story of the recitation of The Lord's Prayer, for example, is still told in various forms. The story of the drunk who only said, "Your worship's wise," reappeared as a story of a drunken Indian, and the story of the drunkard who was warned to quit drinking or lose his sight is also one that is still told. The story of "Kaniserstane" has survived in America in a very attentuated form that has lost all of its sentimentality. It was published in 1811 in Johann Peter Hebel's Schatzkastlein des Rheinischen Hausfreundes *in a form much more similar to the* Franklin's Legacy *version.*

Included in this chapter are a few "diversions" of the sort that might have been published in Games Magazine *if it had existed in the eighteenth century. The kind of word play represented by "A Winter Evening's Job" has experienced a recent revival of interest.*

A. Humor with a Message

Four things should never flatter us; familiarity with the great, the caresses of women, the smiles of our enemies, nor a warm day in winter, for these things are not of long duration. (*The Farmer's Almanack-...for...1793* (24847))

Some go to church just for a walk,
Some go there to laugh and talk;
Some go there for speculation,

Some go there for observation,
Some go there to meet a lover
Some the impulse of't discover;
Some go there to meet a friend,
Some go there the time to spend,
Some go to learn the parson's name,
Some go there to wound his fame,
Many go there to doze and nod,
But few go there to worship God.
(*The Virginia and Farmer's Almanac, for . . . 1793* (24971))

Mahomet Bey, King of Tunis, was dethroned by his subjects; but, having the reputation of the philosopher's stone, he was restored by the Dey of Algiers, upon promising to communicate the secret to him. Mahomet sent a plow with great pomp and ceremony, intimating that agriculture is the strength of a kingdom, and that the only philosopher's stone is a *good crop*, which may be easily converted to gold. (*The New England Almanack . . . for . . . 1793* (25022))

Two gentlemen disputing about religion in Bason's coffe-house, London, said one of them, "I wonder Sir, you should talk of religion, when I'll hold you five guineas you can't say the Lord's Prayer."—"Done," (says the other), "and Johnny Wilkies here shall hold the stakes." The money being deposited, the gentleman began with, "I believe in God," and so went cleverly through the Creed, instead of the Lord's Prayer. "Well," (said the other), "I own I have lost: but I did not think he could have done it." (*The Town and Country Almanack, for . . . 1798* (33203))

People who are resolved to please always at all events, frequently overshoot themselves, and render themselves ridiculous by being *too good*— A lady going to eat *plumb cake* and *candle* at a friend's house one morning, ran to the cradle to see the *fine boy*, as soon as she came in. Unfortunately the *cat* had taken up the baby's place; but before she could give herself time to see her mistake, she exclaimed with uplifted eyes and hands, "Oh! What a sweet child! the very *picture of its father*" (*The Farmer's, Merchant's and Mechanic's Almanack: or, The Register of Maine . . . for . . . 1799* (34394))

In the old Grecian times there was a strange man of the commonwealth of Athens, who was never at rest in any permanent situation; but would almost continually ramble about the world. A friend one day asked him whether he ever intended to quit his rambling mode of life? "Yes," answered the Traveller—"I will settle as soon as I can find a country where reputation and credit is in the hands of honest men, and where merit will constitute consequence."—"I fear then" (said the other) "that you will die before you come to the end of your travels." (*The New Jersey and New York Almanac for . . . 1799* (34542))

A wild young fellow was going abroad: His mother took him up into her closet, telling him she had a precious treasure to deposit in his hands, and after many grave admonitions produced the Bible, handsomely bound in two volumes; and to crown all, advised him to consult and search the scriptures. Little did the youth know how precious the volumes were; but you shall hear. On his return from sea, the old lady one day took him aside, and hoped he had remembered the last instruction she had given him: "Yes," he could very honestly say he had taken care of the Bible. To prove his respect and obedience, he runs upstairs to his own room, and returns instantly, with the two volumes safe and sound.

The good lady pulls off one cover: "Rather too clean, my dear." "O madam, I took great care of them: the second volume is equally fair." She shakes her head; intimating her suspicions that they had not been read so often as she wished: Then opened the first volume, and, lo! a ten pound note is found; the second volume displays a second note, and of twice the value. She was confounded; and so was her son: and regrets that he did not search the scriptures. (*The Columbian Almanac: or, The North American Calendar, for . . . 1800* (35321))

A young nobleman returned from Paris, where he spent the greater part of his fortune, and had acquired nothing but a complete knowledge of all the taverns, brothels, coffee and gaming-houses of that city; soon after his arrival he petitioned the King of Prussia to give him some lucrative post. In answer to his petition, he received a royal official cover, which inclosed, to the great surprise and disappointment of the young gentleman. *The Ace of Diamonds.* (*Isaiah Thomas's Massachusetts, Connecticut, Rhode-Island, Newhampshire and Vermont Almanack . . . for . . . 1800* (36413))

B. Money, Poverty and Miserliness

An usurer was earnestly intreating a preacher strongly to censure usury. The preacher, thinking the usurer was willing to be converted; "Ah! sir," said he, "I perceive in you the happy effects of the grace of God."

"You do not understand me," said the usurer. "There are so many usurers in the town, that I can get nothing; if by your preachings you could make them leave off the trade, I should have alone all the customers." (*Father Abraham's Almanack for . . . 1779* (16050))

A courtier being very sick and much indebted, told his confessor that the only favor he had to ask of God was to prolong his life till he cold pay all his debts. "That is a good motive," replied the confessor, "and it is to be hoped that God will hear your prayer." "If God would do me that favor," said the sick man, in turning himself towards one of his friends, "I should be very certain never to die." (*Father Abraham's Almanack for* . . .*1779* (16050))

An old Miser bid his son observe what Solomon said, which was, " *Always to keep a penny in his pocket.*" But his son said, " *he did not remember that Solomon said any such thing;*" the miser replied, "*Then Solomon was not so wise as he took him to be.*" (*An Almanack, for*. . .*1791* (22378))

A notorious miser, having heard a very eloquent charitable sermon. "this sermon," said he, "strongly proves the necessity of alms, I had almost a mind to beg." (*The Columbian Almanack, for*. . . *1791* (22410))

A Frenchman wanting a lodging, but having no money to pay for it, depended on his wit for a supply; so went into an inn, where he called for a supper and had a bed for the night. The bill came to him in the morning, but our hero ingenuously confessed he had no money, but Boniface would not be thus bamboozled, and swore that he would keep him till he paid.

"Oh, den," (says the Frenchman) "If you will keep me dill I pay, me vill never pay; for me love goot keeping, and me vill love it all de days of my life."

However, Boniface being very rough, poor Monsieur [   ] to exert his wit, and get clear off.

"Don't be angry, Monsieur, don't: dough me has not de money to pay de reckoning, me can do you a bit of service, vich will be all de same as money. Me see you be troubled with de rat, now give me de reckoning, and me will give you a receipt in French—Do you understand de French?"

No, I don't," cried Boniface surlily.

"Well, dat'r no matter, you vill easily find de friend dat vill—Me could write in de English tongue, but me can't."

The Frenchman, after saying this, took pen and ink, and having written a few French lines, gave it to the landlord, who, glad to have any thing for his money, received it with readiness.

Some days after, the rats multiplied so, that Boniface was resolved to try the virtue of this recipe; and having by chance found a gentleman in the tap room that understood French, he begged him to translate the recipe, which he did in the following manner, to the great astonishment of the landlord, and the loud laugh of the company.

"When the rats come, take six boiled eggs, half a pint of wine, small beer, and when they have eat heartily, charge them five shillings for their supper, and they will never come any more." (*The Rhode-Island Almanack, for... 1792*(23830))

A miser being dead and fairly interred, came to the banks of the river Styx, desiring to be carried over, along with the other ghosts. Charon demands his fare, and is surprised to see the miser, rather than pay it, throw himself into the river and swim over to the other side, notwithstanding all the clamour and opposition that could be made to him. All hell was in an uproar; and each of the judges was meditating some punishment suitable to a crime of such dangerous consequences. "Shall he be chained to the rock along with Prometheus? Or tremble below the precipice in company with the Danaides? Or assist Sisyphus in rolling his stone?" "No," says Minos, "none of these, we must invent some severer punishment, let him be sent back to the earth, to see the use his heirs are making of his riches." (*The Federal Almanack for... 1795* (28065))

C. Tyrants and Philosophers

A Sultan and A Dervise

A sultan, amusing himself with walking observed a dervise sitting with a human skull: Not observing his majesty, the reverend old man was looking very earnestly at the skull, and appeared to be in a profound reverie. His attitude and manner surprised the sultan, who approached him, and demanded the cause of his being so deeply engaged in reflection. "Sire" (said the Dervise) "this skull was presented to me this morning, and I have been endeavouring in vain, to discover whether it is the skull of a powerful monarch, like yourself, or a poor Dervise like myself." (*An Astronomical Diary...for...1789* (21480))

An Arabian philosopher was once at the court of a certain king, who was as much distinguished for his injustice as his despotism. This king, agreeably to his characteristic features, was desirous of irritating the sage by some of his insults. To this end he positively affirmed that, in the infernal regions was a "mill for the sole purpose of grinding the heads of the learned;" and then demanded of the venerable philosopher, if it was not so, He, in his turn, replied with a firmness and dignity worthy of the highest eulogium, "Yes; but it is the blood of tyrants which makes the mill turn." (*The United States Almanac, for... 1799*(34546))

D. Gallows Humor

Two brothers coming once to be executed for some enormous crime, the eldest was turned off first, without speaking one word: the other mounted the ladder, began to harrangue the crowd, whose ears were attentively open to hear him, expecting some confession from him. "Good people," says he, "my brother hangs before my face, and you see what a lamentable *spectacle* he makes; in a few moments I shall be turned off too, and then you will see *a pair of spectacles.*" (*Father Hutchins Revived...for...1793* (24416))

One of those wretches, who, having overcome every principle of honesty, affect likewise to disregard the feelings of nature was condemned to be hanged. When under the gallows he uttered many profane and profligate bravadoes; and at last as the moment of execution arrived, he boldly asked the hangman, *if he had any commands for the next world.* Ketch, tying the noose very deliberately, replied—"Yes, my friend—I will trouble you with a line." (*An Astronomical Diary, or Almanack, for...1796* (29493))

One, when the hangman came to put the halter about his neck desired him not to bring the rope too near his throat; "For I am," says he, "so ticklish about that place, I shall hurt myself so with laughing, that it will go near to throttle me." (*Pope's Massachusetts, Rhode-Island, Connecticut, New Hampshire and Vermont Almanac, for...1797* (31028))

An old German, on his way to the gallows was smoking his pipe very deliberately and unconcerned, and continued so after his arrival until a few minutes before he was turned off, when taking his pipe out of his mouth, he stuck it through the button holes of his coat with the same deliberation; the cart being drawn from under him, his weight parted the rope, and as he fell broke his pipe. The old man gets up, and looking round with much perplexity, exclaimed, "there, now you broke mine pipe, mit you dam nonsense." (*The American Almanac, for...1798* (31836))

As a pretty large number of culprits were going to take their last degree at Tyburn, the wife of one of them pressed through the crowd, and told the sheriff she had come to see her poor husband executed, and begged that he might be hanged first in the morning, as she had great ways to go home. (*The New-York, Connecticut, and New Jersey Almanack-...for...1799* (33390))

E. Merriment as a Way of Life

Epitaph—Translated from the French

Gaily I liv'd, as ease and nature taught,
And spent my little life without a thought;
And am amaz'd that death, that tyrant grim,
Should think of me who never thought of him.
(*An Astronomical Diary...for...1780* (16324))

Epitaph
Life is a jest, and all things show it;
I thought so once, but now I know it.
(*The New England Callendar...for...1793* (24995))

A country squire asked a *Merry Andrew*, why he played the fool?
"For the same reason," says he, "that you do; out of want: You do it for
want of wit—I for want of money." (*An Almanack, for...1798* (32941))

The happiest silly fellow I ever knew, was of the number of those
good-natured creatures that are said to do no harm to any but themselves—
Whenever he fell into any misery, he usually called it seeing life. If his
head was broke by a chairman, or his pocket picked by a sharper, he comforted
himself by imitating the *Hibernian* dialect of the one, or the more fashionable
cant of the other, nothing came amiss to him. His inattention to money
matters had incensed his father to such a degree, that all the intercession
of friends in his favour was fruitless. The old gentleman was on his death-
bed. The whole family, and [Dick] among the number, gathered around
him.—"I leave my second son *Andrew*," said the expiring miser, "my whole
estate, and desire him to be frugal."— *Andrew*, in a sorrowful tone, as is
usual on these occasions, prayed Heaven to prolong his life and health to
enjoy it himself. "I recommend *Simon*, my third son, to the care of his
elder brother, and leave him besides four thousand pounds?"—"Ah! father,"
cried Simon, (in great affliction to be sure) "May Heaven give you life and
health to enjoy it yourself." At last, turning to poor *Dick*, "as for you,
you have always been a sad dog; you'll never come to good, you'll never
be rich; I'll leave you a shilling to buy a halter." "Ah! father," cried *Dick*,
without any emotion, "may heaven give you life and health to enjoy it
yourself."—This was all the trouble the loss of fortune gave this thoughtless
imprudent creature; however, the tenderness of an uncle recompensed the
neglect of a father; and my friend is now not only excessively good-humored,
but completely rich. (*The United States Almanac...for...1798* (33101))

F. Comical Sayings of Children

Some time ago, while a very large proprietor of colliers in the east of Scotland, was instructing his daughter, a child of seven years old, in the doctrine of rewards and punishments she was very inquisitive as to the nature of hell. Upon its being explained to be a gulph of fire, of prodigious extent, where all the wicked were to suffer for their transgressions: after [think]ing a little she exclaimed, "Dear Papa, could you not get the Devil to take his coals from you." (*The Federal Almanack, for...1794* (25472))

A woman gave her [   ] child a cloth to warm while she was otherwise busied. The child held it to the fire; but so near that it changed colour presently and began to look like tinder: Upon which the child called to its mother, "Mamma, is it done enough when it turns brown?" (*Beers's Almanac for...1800* (35164))

G. Insolence

A man who had a very flat nose having sneezed in the presence of a jester; the latter cried out, "God preserve your sight." He who sneezed, being surprized at this wish asked him the reason for it? "Because," replied the wag, "your nose is not fit to wear spectacles." (*Barber's Albany Almanack, for...1789* (21178))

A clamourous beggar following a gentleman who had not then anything to give, but would not tell the beggar so, at last turns back, and says, "a man knows not to whom to be charitable among so many of you, for there are some, who, if a man do not give him something, they will curse him to his face." "O Sir," says the beggar, "you are mistaken in me; I am none of those." "Then," said the gentleman, "go your way, I will try you for once." (*Weatherwise's Almanack for...1795* (28037))

At a musical country meeting, a vocal performer, (who was rather shabby about the *under garments*) being complimented on the power of his voice, vainly threw up his head, and replied, "O Lord, Sir. I can *make any thing of it.*" "Can you indeed?" said a wit in the company: "Why then I'd advise you to *make yourself a pair of breeches of it.*" (*Franklin's Legacy; or, The Lansingburgh Almanack, for...1798* (32690))

H. Drinking

Five Reasons for Drinking
Good wine—a friend—or being dry;
    Or, lest we should be by and by;
Or, any other reason why.

(*An Astronomical Diary: or Almanack, for* . . . *1782* (17202))

A drunken fellow was brought before a justice, and to every question he answered, " *Your worship's wise.*" He was committed to prison and sent for the next morning, and told of his idle talk the night before. "Why, what did I say?" "Why, whatsoever I said," says the justice, "you still said, 'Your worship's wise;' so that I thought you was mad." "Truly," says he, "if I said so, I think I was mad indeed." (*Father Tammany's Almanac, for* . . . *1787* (20160))

A drunkard having but one of his eyes left with drinking, was warned by the physicians to leave off tippling, or else he would lose the other eye also: "Faith," says he, "I care not if I do; for I do confess ingeniously, I have seen enough, but I have not drunk enough." (*Bickerstaff's Genuine Almanack for* . . . *1789* (21593))

A rich farmer having a wife who frequently got intoxicated with cider; in order to deter her from following that practice, told her one day, that the next time she got in that *trim*, he would bury her, and accordingly had a coffin made for her and brought home to his house. Not long after, however the farmer had occasion to go from home, and his wife, not minding his threats, nor regarding the sight of her coffin, took the opportunity of *drinking her fill*; the farmer coming home, found her drunk on the floor; he accordingly had her put into the coffin, and conveyed down cellar, and there waited till she came to her senses; as soon as she came too, and reflecting on her past folly, thinking she had left the terrestrial world, with all its *good juice* of the apple—she began knocking on the side of her coffin, and addressed herself, in an audible voice, in these words—" *Ye inhabitants of this new world, have you here any good cider?*" (*Stoddard's Diary: or, The Columbian Almanack, for* . . . *1797* (30048))

A fellow that used to be drunk, when he came home wallowed about the floor, and said, he paid rent for the house and would lie where he pleased. In one of his frolics he fell into the fire. The maid ran to her mistress, and told her that her master had fallen into the fire, and she could not get him out. "Let him alone," says she, "he *pays rent for the house; let him lie where he pleases!*" (*Franklin's Legacy; or, The New-York and Vermont Almanack for* . . . *1800* (35169))

A veteran toper complained to a celebrated Doctor W. of Boston, that from long use of spiritous liquors, they paled upon his palate, and failed to exhilerate his spirits. The Doctor, in a sportive mood, recommended *Agua Fortis* to him, diluted with water. The toper immediately procured a considerable quantity, and then took it in its crude state; but in a few months it afforded him no more pleasure than New-England rum. Soon after the unfortunate tippler, meeting the Doctor in the street, addressed him thus: "Doctor, the Aqua *Forties* won't do—can't you give me something stronger? Do dear Doctor, for the love of *grog*, let me have a little Aqua Fifties!" (*Franklin's Legacy: or, The New-York and Vermont Almanack for... 1800* (35169))

An honest sober man, not very elegantly dressed, nor of a very winning appearance, happened to call at a tavern, where a company of genuine *soakers* had got possession of the bar-room, and were skin full of the *good-creature*—the eyes of all were turned upon him, and they thought him a fit subject for a jest. One of them accosted him with, "Well friend, what news have you?"—"None at all," said he.—"Then," replied the other, "We can tell you some." "Ah! what is it?" "Why the devil is dead." "Say you so," (replied the man) "then I am sorry for *your* loss, for I perceive he has left a number of poor *fatherless children* behind him." (*Poor Richard Improved: being an Almanack... for...1800* (36277))

Comparisons on Drunkenness

As drunk as an owl; as drunk as a sow; as drunk as a beggar; as drunk as the Devil; as drunk as a Lord.—These are the principal comparisons of drunkenness, and the explanation is as follows: A man is as drunk as an owl when he cannot see; he is as drunk as a sow when he tumbles in the dirt; he is as drunk as a beggar, when he is very impudent; he is as drunk as the Devil, when he is inclined to mischief; and is drunk as a Lord, when he is everything that is bad. (*Hutchins Improved: an Almanac, for...1801* (36927))

I. Puns and Verbal Misunderstandings

A short time prior to Mr. Lunardi's ascension into the atmosphere; a countryman asked a Quaker, whether the report of our *elevated* hero's intention to take such a flight was founded in truth, or whether the inflammable matter possessed the power that had been imputed to it? "Why, truly, Friend," (replied the Quaker), "I cannot justly inform thee; but it is a maxim with me, never to credit *inflammatory rumours and flying reports!*" (*Loudon's Almanack...for...1786* (19499))

An epicure, requested his landlord, to get him a spare rib. The Innkeeper declared, he had none, saving one, and that was a crooked rib, which he should be glad enough to spare. (*Father Tammany's Almanac for... 1793* (25059))

When the late Mr. Webb, the comedian and his wife first applied to Mr. Coleman for an engagement, they declared they had only a small matter, which they mentioned, to live on. "Bless my soul, my poor fat people!" (exclaimed the manager, looking alternately at their prominent bellies) "how do you contrive to make both ends meet?" (*Bickerstaff's New-England Almanack for . . . 1794* (26461))

A man being brought before the Vice Chancellor, on an accusation preferred against him, began to *hawk* and *spit*. On being asked what he meant by such insolence, he said he was come to *clear* himself. (*The Farmer's Almanac, for . . . 1800*(35167))

A young Parisian, travelling to Amsterdam, was attracted by the remarkable beauty of a house near the canal. He addressed a Dutchman, in French, who stood near him in the vessel with, "Pray, Sir, may I ask who that house belongs to?" The Hollander answered him in his own language, *"Ik kan niet verstaan."* (I do not understand you). The Parisian, not doubting but that he was understood, took the Dutchman's answer for the name of the proprietor. "Oh, oh!" said he, "it belongs to Mr. *Kaniserstane.* Well, I am sure he must be very agreeably situated; the house is most charming. I don't know that I ever saw better. A friend of mine has one like it near the river Cloise; but I certainly give this the preference." He added many other observations of the same kind, to which the Dutchman made no answer.

When he arrived at Amsterdam, he saw a most beautiful woman on the quay, walking arm in arm with a gentleman; he asked a person who passed him who that charming lady was. But the man, not understanding French, replied, *" Ik kan niet verstaan."* "What, Sir," replied our traveller, "is that Mr. Kaniserstane's wife, whose house is near the canal? Indeed this gentleman's lot is enviable, to possess such a noble house and so sweet a companion."

The next day, when he was walking out, he saw some trumpeters playing at a gentleman's door, who had got the largest prize in the Dutch lottery. Our Parisian, wishing to be informed of the gentleman's name, it was still answered *" Ik kan niet verstaan."* — "Oh," said he, "this is too great an accession of good fortune! Mr. Kaniserstane proprietor of such a fine house, husband to such a beautiful woman, and to get the largest prize in the lottery! It must be allowed that there are some fortunate men in this world."

About a week after this, our traveller, walking about, saw a very superb burying. He asked whose it was? *" Ik kan niet verstaan,"* replied the person of whom he enquired. "Oh, my God!" exclaimed he, "poor Mr. Kaniserstane, who had such a noble house, such an angelic wife, and the largest prize in the lottery! He must have quitted this world with much regret! But I thought his happiness was too complete to be of long duration." He then went home, reflecting all the way on the instability of human affairs. (*Franklin's Legacy: or, the New-York and Vermont Almanack for...1800* (35169))

At a tea party, where the company was busily engaged in conversation, the lady of the house forgetting to put tea into the pot, filled the cups, and sent them round; when a gentleman, a little waggishly inclined, observed, "You think, Madam, that you have been making tea, when you have only been *making water!*" (*The Virginia and North Carolina Almanac, for...1800* (35239))

A writer in Lloyd's Coffee House, London, being informed that a certain ship in whose fate he was deeply interested, was in jeopardy— exclaimed "Jeopardy! Jeopardy! What part of the world is that in?—Near Gibraltar I suppose [.] I am glad to hear she is in any port, for I thought it was all over with her!" (*An Astronomical Diary, Calendar, or Almanack, for...1800* (36383))

A lady being asked how she liked a gentleman's singing, who had an offensive breath; said, "The words are good, but the air is intolerable." (*The Farmer's Almanac, for...1801* (36925))

A Gentleman who returned from the East Indies, enquired of his neighbour after a former acquaintance of his, who, it seems, had been hanged for forgery. The gentleman was informed that he had made some "speculations," and died soon after. "And did he continue in the grocery line?"—"Oh, no," (answered the other) "he was in quite a different line when he died." (*The Virginia and North Carolina Almanack for...1801* (37046))

Some persons broke into the stable of a troop of horse, and cut off all the tails. A brother officer advised the troop to sell them wholesale;— "For," says he, "you can never retail them." (*The Kentucky Almanac for...1801* (37728))

J. Games, Diversions, etc.

A Rebus from *The Pennsylvania Magazine*
What's fickle as the wind, the French delight
A small disease that's hurtful to the sight:
The words when joined together will express

The greatest charm a female can possess.
(*An Astronomical Diary...for...1780* (16324))
(The answer is "modesty." ed.)

A Rebus
Take the latter four-fifths of an insect's produce,
And a thousand that's shortest set down;
Then prefix this to that, and 'twill shew what's of use
In supporting the country and town.
(*Loudon's Almanack...for...1786* (19499))
(The answer is "money." ed.)

Anagram

If you transpose what ladies wear,	Veil
Twill plainly shew what harlots are:	Vile
Again if you transpose the same,	
You'll see an ancient Hebrew name.	Levi
Change it again, and it will shew	
What all on earth desire to do.	Live
Transpose these letters yet once more,	
What bad men do, you'll then explore.	Evil

(*The Pennsylvania Almanack...for...1787* (20023))

A Winter Evening's Job Recommended to the Curious by S. A.

Friends Sir Friends
stand
I
your
bearing
Disposition
A man to the World
is
contempt
whilst the ambitious
ridiculed
are
& when we are married may
expect XX and eeee

. . . .

Stand   take   to   takings
I   you   throw   my

. . . .

        B   not   yy   nor
                                   nice
           for uc how A fool ub.
The above may be easily understood by
exercising a little Patience.
(*Weatherwise's Town and Country Almanack...for...1787* (20125)) (The
answer may be as follows: "Sir, between friends, I understand your overbearing
disposition. A man to the world is above contempt whilst the ambitious
are under-ridiculed, and when we are married may expect kisses and ease.
I understand you undertake to overthrow my undertakings. Be not too wise
nor over nice, for you see how big a fool you be." ed.)

    Acrostick
Whistling winds, frost and flowers
Icicles and snowy towers,
New-born clouds and aether low'es
These and more are winter sprights,
Evenings dark and dismal nights,
Rural storms and dreary sights.
(*The Columbian Almanack...for...1789* (20958))
(The first letter of each line spells out "winter." ed.)

Just thirty days hath the month of September,
The same may be said of June, April, November;
All the rest of the months have thirty and one,
Except that short month February alone,
Which to itself claimeth just eight and a score,
And every leap year we give it one more.
(*Barber's Albany Almanack, for...1789* (21178))

    K. Fashion and Pride

      Mr. Modish having sagaciously smelt at the breech of a rabbit, wiped
his nose, gave a shrug of some dissatisfaction, and then informed the company
that it was not absolutely a bad one, but that he heartily wished it had
been kept a day longer: "Ah," said Sir Titbit with an emphasis, "a rabbit
must be kept." "And with the guts in it, too," added Colonel Trencher,
"or the Devil could not eat it."—Here the Maitre d'hotel interposed and
said, "that they eat their rabbits much sooner now than they used to at
Paris." "Are you sure of it?" said Mr. Modish with some vivacity. "Yes,"
replied the Maitre d'hotel "the cook had a letter about it last night." "I
am glad on it," rejoined Mr. Modish, "for to tell you the truth, Gemmen,
I naturally love to eat my meat before it stinks." (*The Columbian
Almanack...for...1791* (22912))

Two macaronies running accidentally against each other, they made a thousand apologies, hoping neither was hurt. "Hurt!" cried a gentleman, "two puffs of wind might as well be bruised, as such hollow animals as you are." (*The Farmer's Almanack, for...1797* (30400))

J. Stories of historical figures

Jonathan Swift

Early in life, Dean Swift having preached an assize sermon in Ireland, was afterwards invited to dine with the judges; in the course of the sermon, he was very severe upon the counsel for pleading for people against their own consciences. After dinner, a young barrister, not knowing whom he had to deal with, thought he would be even with the parson; and having said a great many sweet things against the clergy, which the Dean took notice of, at length said, that if the devil was to die, he did not doubt but that a parson might be found for money to preach his funeral sermon. "Yes, Sir!" said Swift, "I would willingly be the man myself, and *give the devil his due,* as I have *his children* this day." (*The Farmer's Almanack,...for...1799* (34654))

Dean Swift being once travelling through England on foot, came to a market town one evening, where he proposed putting up for the night. As there had been a fair the preceeding day, the town was crowded with strangers, and it was not without the utmost difficulty he at last procured a lodging in a miserable inn, upon condition a country farmer should be his bed fellow. The dean, it is well known, could never endure a bed fellow; but upon this occasion thought it proper to conceal his chagrin, and trust to some lucky thought to rid himself of the farmer's company. After they had been some time in bed together, the farmer began to talk, informing his companion that he had made some pretty clever bargains that day in some purchases at vendue—"Ah, for myself," said the dean, in a hoarse hollow voice, "I must confess that I have had but very indifferent luck, not having tucked up above seven this assize."—"Why, what business do you follow?" cried the farmer. "I am the hangman of the next county," replied the dean. "You the hangman," shrieked the country man in a fright. "Yes," said the dean, "and expect to hang nine more next Saturday at Tyburn, one of whom is to be drawn and quartered." The fellow waited for no further reply, but flew out of his bed with the violence of a man in fits, burst open the door, tumbled down stairs in the dark, and awakened the landlord with the noise, who demanded what was the matter.—"Matter," cried the farmer, "by all the devils in hell, I have been put to bed with the hangman, and never discovered it till this instant: is this the way you use strangers; for God's sake open the door, and let me get into the street." (*Weatherwise's Massachusetts, Connecticut, Rhodeisland, Newhampshire and Vermont Almanack, for . . . 1799*(34969))

Anecdote of Dean Swift

This singular character had been famous for his writings; being of a satyrical turn, his mark was chiefly the right reverends of the church; and scarce a clergyman of any note escaped being lampooned by him, the bishop of Dublin being excepted, with whom the dean was always on good terms—the bishop never failing to send, every week, some handsome present to the dean; and, that it might appear the better, always sent his butler with it.—One day a tenant of the bishop's caught a wonderful large salmon, which he made a present of to the bishop: the bishop says to his butler, "take this salmon directly to the dean, with my compliments, and beg his acceptance, and inquire after his health." The butler, who had been many times with presents to the dean, and who, by the bye, never gave any money to any one who brought a present; nor had his servants orders to ask them to take any refreshment, or even sit down; finding it a dark and gloomy day, and very dirty, did not much admire a job of carrying a salmon of twenty or thirty pounds weight, near five miles to the dean's house, began to grumble while he was in the kitchen, and wished the dean and the salmon were both at the devil, for if he took it he was sure of getting nothing by it. The bishop's post boy said, "I suppose you have had many a bright guinea from the dean, as you always take the presents to him, but you pretend not to have received any thing." The butler replied, "If you will take the salmon in this basket, I will give you half a crown for your trouble, as it is a nasty dirty day, and a long way off; and will lay you half a guinea that the dean will not give you either money or refreshment;" which wager the post-boy agreed to, and set off. He arrived at the dean's door, all muddy, cold and hungry, and knocking at the door; the porter opened it. The lad said, "is the dean at home?" The porter replied, "Yes, but he cannot see any person; he is in his study." "Oh, very well," said the boy, "if he cannot let me deliver to himself a handsome present I have for him in this basket, I must take it back again." The porter said, "Stop, I will speak to him;" on which he went to the dean and said, "Please, your reverence, there is a post-boy at the door, who has something in a basket for you, which he will not deliver but to you personally." The dean replied, "Well, send him in." The lad neither pulled his hat off, nor wiped his shoes, but said, "Are you the dean?" to which he replied, "Yes, I am." The boy says "There, take this from the bishop of Dublin," and puts the basket on the table, and went out as he came in: and did not offer to shut the door. When the boy had got nearly out, the dean rings his bell violently, and says to his man, "Tell that unmannerly dog to come back here." The lad was called, who came in as before. The dean says to the lad, "How long have you been with the bishop?" The boy replied, "Near three years." The dean says, "I am surprised you have learnt no manners. Come here. I will learn you a little; here, take my cap and morning gown, and sit down in this great chair, and you for a little time shall be the dean, and I will be the bishop's post-boy, and shew you how you should behave on this occasion." The dean takes the basket under his arm out of the room, shuts the door, and knocks twice with his hand; the boys says, "Come in." The dean makes a low bow, and says, "Please your reverence, I brought a present of a salmon, with my master, the lord bishop of Dublin's compliments, who desired me at the same time to inquire of your reverence's health." The boy says, "Very well, my lad, put it down on this table." The boy rings the bell, up comes the butler to the dean; the boy says, "it is a nasty, dirty cold day: I suppose you are cold, hungry, and tired. Take this lad down; give him something to eat and drink; give him half a guinea for his trouble." The dean finding himself outwitted, said, "Give me my gown and cap," which he did, and sat down, and said to the butler, "Give the lad half a guinea for me, take him down, it is a cold, dirty day; let him clean himself, and give him something comfortable to eat and drink." The lad went below, got money, victuals, and drink, and warmed himself by a good fire, returned to the bishop's, told the story to the bishop's butler, and, of course, won the wager. (*Stoddard's Diary: or, the Columbia Almanack, for . . . 1800* (35173))

Other figures

A zealous officer of Cromwell's came to him, and told him he had fallen into bad company, where he had the mortification to hear his highness spoken of in a very scandalous manner.

"Aye," says Oliver, "man, what did they say?"

"I am ashamed, an't please your Highness, to repeat it."

"Tell, tell," says Oliver.

"Why an't please your Highness, a rascal had the impudence to say, your Highness might kiss his arse."

"How! how! what sort of a man was he?"

"Oh!" says the officer, "he was but a poor beggarly fellow."

"Oho!" says the Protector, "when you see him again, tell him, he may kiss mine."(*Father Tammany's Almanac for . . . 1793* (25059))

Socrates, when under sentence of death, was visited by a friend, who expressed great grief for him, that he was condemned to die *innocent*. "What," said Socrates, with a smile, "would you have me die guilty?" (*An Almanack, for . . . 1798* (32941))

Dr. Middleton, author of the life of Cicero, was visited in his last illness by his Physician, who found him propped up by a bed chair and writing with a desk before him. On seeing the Doctor, he asked him, how long he could live? The Doctor replied, "perhaps twenty-four hours." "Well then," said he coolly, "I shall not have time to finish what I am about." So he ordered his chair to be taken away, and resigned himself quietly to his fate. (*Greenleaf's New-York, Connecticut, and New-Jersey Almanac . . . for . . . 1800* (35171))

Of Diogenes the Cynic
While Diogenes was discoursing accurately against anger, a waggish youth to make trial, whether he would abide by his doctrine, spit in his face—this he bore wisely and mildly—"I am not, indeed," says he, "angry, but I have some doubts, whether I ought not to be angry!" (*The New-Jersey and Pennsylvania Almanac, for . . . 1800* (36305))

Des Cartes, when at table, greedily partook of all the choicest dishes which appeared. One day, a nobleman, remarkable for his ignorance, being in the company, and desirous, as he supposed, to rally des Cartes for acting in a manner which he judged incompatible with his character; "I always," said he, "considered you Philosophers as men of remarkable temperance, who treated the gratification of the passions as a matter unworthy of notice." "Hold your peace, Friend," replied des Cartes: "In justice to the almighty wisdom of God, we are not to suppose he made good things only for Dunces!" (*Dickson's Balloon Almanac, for . . . 1801* (37325))

Notes

Introduction

[1]George Lyman Kittredge, *The Old Farmer and His Almanack* (Cambridge: Harvard University Press, 1920, Reprint, New York: B. Blom, 1967).

[2]Robb Sagendorph, *America and her Almanacs: Wit, Wisdom and Weather* (Boston: Yankee-Little Brown, 1970).

[3]Stowell, Marion Barber, Early American Almanacs: The Colonial Weekday Bible (New York: Burt Franklin, 1977).

[4]Robert K. Dodge, "Didatic Humor in the Almanacs of Early America," *Journal of Popular Culture*, 5 (Winter 1971) 592-605.

[5]Jon Stanley Wenrick, "Indians in Almanacs, 1783-1815," *Indian Historian*, 8 (Winter 1977) 36-42.

[6]Robert K. Dodge, "The Irish Comic Stereotype in the Almanacs of the Early Republic," *Eire-Ireland*, 19 (Fall, 1984) 111-120.

[7]Richard Dorson, *Folklore and Fakelore* (Cambridge: Harvard University Press, 1976) 277.

[8] *The Virginia Almanac*, for. . .1799 (Winchester: Bowen, 1798).

[9]Gershon Legman, *Rationale of the Dirty Joke* (New York: Grove Press, 1968) 377.

[10]Charles Evans, *American Bibliography* (New York: Peter Smith, 1941-1959). Gordon K. Shipton, *Early American Imprints* (Worcester, Mass: American Antiquarian Society, A Readex Microprint edition, 1955).

Chapter One

[1]Nehemiah Strong, *An Astronomical Diary, Kalender or Almanack, for. . .1791* (Hartford: Babcock, 1790). All further citations of almanacs will be made in parentheses within the text. The Evans numbers will be given in lieu of detailed publication information. These numbers provide access to *Early American Imprints*. and prevent confusion of almanacs with similar titles and publication dates and places. At least five *Astronomical Diaries* were published for 1791, for example, At least two of those were published in Hartford and list Nehemiah Strong as the author. The one which contains the Putnam story is Evans #22915.

Chapter Two

[1]Richard Dorson, *America in Legend: Folklore from the Colonial Period to the Present* (New York: Pantheon Books, 1973), 111-116.

Chapter Four

[1]Noah Webster and Chauncy Goodrich, *An American Dictionary of the English Language* (Chicago: Loomis and Co., 1890), 155.